THE FEDERALIST PAPERS

Alexander Hamilton
John Jay
James Madison

AUTHORED by Brittany Nelson and Christopher Higgins (second revision 09/15/2011)
UPDATED AND REVISED by Elizabeth Weinbloom

COVER DESIGN by Table XI Partners LLC
COVER PHOTO by Olivia Verma and © 2005 GradeSaver, LLC

BOOK DESIGN by Table XI Partners LLC

Published by GradeSaver LLC, www.gradesaver.com

First published in the United States of America by GradeSaver LLC. 2011

GRADESAVER, the GradeSaver logo and the phrase "Getting you the grade since 1999" are registered trademarks of GradeSaver, LLC

ISBN 978-1-60259-283-4

Printed in the United States of America

For other products and additional information please visit

Table of Contents

Table of Contents

Table of Contents

Table of Contents

Table of Contents

Table of Contents

Biography of Hamilton, Alexander (1755-1804)

This principal architect of the Federalist Papers is exceptional and enigmatic among figures of the revolutionary period. Belatedly and only grudgingly admitted to the canon of great American thinkers, Hamilton's importance as an early nationalist, a leading exponent of Federalism, and a political and financial visionary in the critical post-revolutionary years only fully came to light in the mid-twentieth century, as scholars viewing the financial and administrative histories of the early United States began to reconsider his achievements. He is best remembered as an outspoken proponent of strong central government and for his authorship of the Federalist Papers, but his many other achievements and characteristics make him a difficult figure to grasp. He was a brilliant, influential, and well-respected patriot, but he was also a fiercely ambitious self-promoter and opportunist, criticized for his arrogance as much as he was admired for his intellect and drive.

Born in the small Caribbean island of Nevis in 1755, then part of the British West Indies, Hamilton's humble origins made him an unlikely candidate for post-revolutionary prominence on the continent. His father's mediocrity in business and his mother's early death seemed to limit his possibilities, but his maternal relations' recognized the young man's promise at an early age, and afforded Hamilton enough support to relocate to Boston in 1772 at the age of 17. Shortly thereafter he moved to New York and enrolled in King's College, now Columbia University. His intellectual pursuits soon gave way to a desire to promote the revolution. "I wish there were a war," he confided in a letter to a friend. Between an inspirational speech he made in the "fields" of New York City (City Hall Park), and his authorship of two pamphlets decrying Loyalist arguments, a young revolutionary was born. When conflict broke out, he assumed the role of artillery captain and was noted for his service in the battles of Long Island, White Plains, Trenton, and Princeton. General Nathanael Green recommended Hamilton to George Washington, who in March 1777 took him on as an aide-de-camp and personal secretary. After a dispute with the commander-in-chief caused him to resign, he continued his distinction in service commanding infantry at the battle of Yorktown.

After the war ended, Hamilton settled in New York and embarked upon a distinguished legal career. In this period he completed a stint in the Continental Congress in 1782-3 and developed his law practice, but most notable was the key role he played in the 1786 Annapolis Convention which addressed issues in interstate commerce. It was his argumentation in the latter convention that highlighted the shortcomings of the government established under the Articles of Confederation. Importantly, it established his reputation as the foremost proponent of a strong central government for the newly independent colonies, paving the public intellectual foundation for the substantial architectonic changes he would engineer in the federal government while in office. He attended the Constitutional Convention in Philadelphia in 1787, but his outspoken support of strong government, particularly his proposition of electing a president for life, placed him in the minority. At any rate, the power of his two fellow New York delegates, both Anti-Federalists, ensured his inefficacy; they outvoted him two-to-one on nearly every issue.

In spite of his inability to effect much of an influence at Philadelphia, Hamilton nevertheless became the Constitution's most vocal supporter in New York during the ratification debates. Even though the document probably fell short of his desires, he spared no effort in promoting it during a critical period in arguably the most critical state. The primary means by which he did this was of course the publication of the Federalist Papers. Exactly how many of the anonymous letters comprising this work were written by Hamilton is in dispute, but it appears he wrote at least 51 of the 85 total tracts. The essays were less useful convincing voters directly of the Constitution's necessity, but they became a staple for public debaters in Virginia and New York. They clearly helped enhance the force of Federalist arguments in the key debates, bargains, and negotiations leading up to ratification.

It is in the Federalist Papers that the political pragmatism and nationalism of Hamilton are most evident. He makes his most convincing arguments for a strong American state here, and his commentary on subjects from foreign affairs to public administration. His ardent nationalism and occasionally dogmatic personality color his writings, which determine in large part the character of the entire document. Even though James Madison penned Federalist 10 and 51, perhaps the most famous essays in the collection, Hamilton's contributions to the volume's development were probably paramount. It was Hamilton who enlisted Madison and Jay to the task in the first place; when Madison and Jay departed from the project, Hamilton continued writing tirelessly. He probably exerted more influence on his companion's work than they upon him; the nature of his personality probably dictated the inevitability of such an outcome.

Following ratification, Washington appointed Hamilton the first Secretary of the Treasury. The nation's finances still in disarray after the war and independence, Hamilton's proposals to pay the foreign debt and improve public credit were hotly debated in Congress. Among them were certain provisions, particularly federal assumption of state debts and the establishment of a central bank, that drew considerable resentment for the extra short-term burdens they would place upon the recovery effort. The public's weak grasp of political economy must have made Hamilton's proposals appear unnecessarily difficult. In spite of this, the reforms ultimately won out. Historians have since pointed to them as key factors in helping sustain the early American state, particularly through its confrontation with Britain in the War of 1812.

The first Secretary of the Treasury also had considerable influence over foreign policy. He convinced Washington to adopt a policy of neutrality toward wars in Europe, in spite of strong public desires to support France. In addition, his instructions laid the groundwork for the 1794 agreement with England now known as Jay's Treaty, which settled longstanding disputes and provided for the evacuation of British troops on American borders. He was appointed Inspector General of the Army under President Adams, at Washington's urging. His disputes with Adams during this period were key causes of cleavages in the Federalist party and the party's subsequent defeat at the hands of the Republican party in the election of 1800.

Returning intermittently to his law practice through the 1790s, the hiatus from public life Hamilton took after the election of 1800 was cut short by an untimely and infamous death at the hands of Aaron Burr. Owing in part to Hamilton's electoral support of Thomas Jefferson over Burr, who he considered dangerous, Burr challenged Hamilton to a duel on July 11, 1804 at Weehauken, New Jersey. Even though some evidence indicates Burr intended only to maim Hamilton, a mortal wound he dealt to the latter's midsection resulted in death on the following day.

Conclusion

Hamilton's legacy is most easily recognized in his authorship of the Federalist Papers. There, his role as a proponent for strong central government and his nationalistic fervor are most evident. But his contributions to public finance and public administration while Secretary of the Treasury, only recently rediscovered by scholars, must rank among his most important achievements. Historian of United States public administration Leonard D. White has called him "the greatest administrative genius of his generation in America, and one of the greatest administrators of all time." Perhaps begrudged a prominent place among the founding fathers for his attention to pragmatic concerns over ideals, Hamilton's role in ensuring the survival and prosperity of the early republic was clearly crucial.

In spite of this, Hamilton remains an elusive figure. Historians are often at a loss to explain his self-aggrandizing and opportunistic tendencies, qualities which do not flatter the statesman in the way his life achievements do. He left enormous volumes of letters, tracts, and personal papers with which historians have reconstructed his role in the early republic, but our understanding of Hamilton's psychology, the origins of his professional aspirations, and the nature of his intellectual prowess are less clear. Certainly a key personality in American history, Alexander Hamilton's personal life probably deserves more scholarly attention than it has received thus far.

Biography of Jay, John (1745-1829)

John Jay was born into an old New York family on December 12th, 1745, and educated at King's College (which later became Columbia University), where he graduated in 1764. In 1768, he was admitted to the bar. Representing the point of view of the American merchants in protesting British restrictions on the commercial activities of the colonies, he was elected to the Continental Congress in 1774 and again in 1775. Jay did not favor independence from Britain. Thomas Jefferson noted his absence from the signing of the Declaration of Independence. However, once the revolution was undertaken Jay was an ardent supporter of the new nation. He drafted the first constitution of New York State and was appointed chief justice of the state in 1777. In the following year he was again elected to the Continental Congress and was chosen as its president.

The Congress sent Jay to Spain in 1779 to obtain its endorsement of the independence of the colonies and a loan in support of the Revolutionary War. Unfortunately, Spain would provide neither. In Paris in 1782, he was one of the commissioners (with Benjamin Franklin and John Adams) who negotiated the Treaty of Paris with Great Britain, ending the American Revolution. While the party was instructed to insist only on independence of the colonies and defer to France on all other matters, France was occupied with fighting Spain in Gibraltar, which showed no signs of ending. Privately, Jay, Franklin, and Adams negotiated a treaty far better than the U.S. Congress could ever have hoped for. Britain guaranteed the independence of the Untied States, ceded the entire territory east of the Mississippi River, and gave the Americans valuable fishing rights in the North Atlantic.

From 1784 to 1789, Jay was secretary for foreign affairs. The ineffectiveness of the Articles of Confederation led him to become a proponent of a strong national government. After the Constitution was ratified, George Washington nominated John Jay as the chief justice, and he was confirmed two days later. George Washington had chosen wisely in selecting the first chief justice. Jay had always been widely respected as a just and reasonable man. His stewardship of the court only improved his standing and, not incidentally, did much to establish the Supreme Court as a reasoned and honorable institution. In 1794, however, when war with Britain threatened due to controversies over the Treaty of Paris, Jay was appointed by Washington to negotiate a settlement, even while serving as Supreme Court Justice.

On his return, Jay found that he had been elected as governor of New York in 1795, a surprise to him as he was not even asked if he would serve. Jay was forced to retire from the Supreme Court, though he would not have chosen to do so, because his friends in New York had called him to service. Though the fury of public reaction to Jay's treaty marred his first term, he was reelected and proved to be a most popular and productive governor.

John Jay survived his wife and several of his children. The last years of his life were not comfortable. Though he was wealthy and had the support of his children, his health was poor. He died on May 17th, 1829, in the comfort of his home.

Biography of Madison, James (1751-1836)

James Madison was born into planter aristocracy at Port Conway, Virginia on March 16, 1751, the oldest of ten children. He received his early education from his mother, tutors, and a private school. In 1771 he graduated from the College of New Jersey (which became Princeton) where he demonstrated special interest in government and the law. He stayed for a year of postgraduate study in theology, considering the ministry.

Undecided on a profession, Madison returned to his family's estate of Montpelier and embraced the patriot cause, and state and local politics became his primary interest. In 1775 he served on the Orange County committee of safety; the next year at the Virginia convention which, besides advocating various Revolutionary steps, framed the Virginia constitution; in 1776-77 in the House of Delegates; and in 1778-80 in the Council of State. His ill health precluded any military service.

In 1780 Madison was chosen to represent Virginia in the Continental Congress (1780-83 and 1786-88). Although originally the youngest delegate, he played a major role in the deliberations of that body. Meantime, in the years 1784-86, he had again sat in the Virginia House of Delegates. Madison was clearly the preeminent figure at the convention. Some of the delegates favored an authoritarian central government; others, retention of state sovereignty; and most occupied positions in the middle of two extremes. Madison, who was rarely absent and whose Virginia Plan was in large part the basis of the Constitution, advocated a strong government, though many of his proposals were rejected. Despite his poor speaking abilities, he took the floor over 150 times. His journal of the convention is the best record of the event and he played a key part in guiding the Constitution through the Continental Congress.

In the U.S. House of Representatives (1789-97), Madison helped write and ensure the passage of the Bill of Rights. He also assisted in organizing the executive department and creating a system of federal taxation. As leaders of the opposition to Hamilton's polices, he and Jefferson founded the Democratic-Republican party. In 1794 Madison married a widow 16 years his junior, Dolly Payne Todd, who had a son: they, however, had no children of their own. Madison spent the 1797-1801 in semiretirement, but in 1798 he wrote the Virginia Resolution, which attacked the Alien and Sedition Acts. While he served as Secretary of State (1801-9), his wife often served as Jefferson's hostess.

In 1809, James Madison succeeded Jefferson as President of the United States. Like the first three Presidents, Madison was immersed in the ramifications of European wars, which soon led to the War of 1812. The war, for which the United States was ill-prepared, concluded in 1814 when the inconclusive Treaty of Ghent, which merely restored prewar conditions, was signed. Thanks to Andrew Jackson's spectacular victory at the Battle of New Orleans in January 1815, most Americans believed they had won, creating a spike in nationalism during Madison's last years in office.

In retirement after his second term, Madison managed Montpelier but continued to be active in public affairs. He devoted long hours to editing his journal of the Constitutional Convention, which the government published four years after his death. He served as co-chairman of the Virginia constitutional convention of 1829-80 and as rector of the University of Virginia during the period 1826-36. Writing newspaper articles defending the administration of his successor President Monroe, he also acted as his foreign policy adviser. Madison spoke out in support of mildly protective tarries, the National Bank, and, most importantly, the power of the union against nullification. Madison's health slowly declined, forcing him more and more to be a silent observer. He died June 28, 1836, the last survivor of the founders of the American Republic.

About The Federalist Papers

The Federalist Papers is a treatise on free government in peace and security. It is the outstanding American contribution to the literature on constitutional democracy and federalism, and a classic of Western political thought.

The Federalist Papers were written in support of the ratification of the Constitution. While modern day readers might see it as inevitable, the Constitution was a revolutionary step. In Philadelphia, the delegates rebelled against the existing Articles of Confederation and looked to the states, not the existing government, for ratification and approval of the new government. Because of the revolutionary nature of the new constitution, arguments were necessary to rationalize the response to the new emergencies. After the convention, therefore, Tench Coxe became the coordinator in Philadelphia for those who supported the constitution while George Mason became the coordinator for New York for those who opposed it. Hundreds and hundreds of letters were written regarding the constitution, "Cato" and "The Federal Farmer" attacked while "Caeser" replied. Both George Washington and Ben Franklin, probably the two most influential men in the country, supported the Constitution.

Pennsylvania, Massachusetts, Virginia, and New York were the states critical to the success or failure of the Constitution. Of these four states, New York by far was the state where the success of the constitution was in the most doubt. The state's delegation did not approve the draft in Philadelphia because two of its three delegates left during the protest and abandoned Alexander Hamilton without a vote. Governor Clinton, the leading figure in New York politics, opposed the new government: New York had become an independent nation under the Articles of Confederation, making itself rich through tariffs on trade with its neighboring states.

Quickly, Alexander Hamilton decided that a massive propaganda campaign was necessary in New York, more than in any other state. This new plan entailed a saturation theory, a sustained barrage of arguments appearing in newspapers four times a week. Because of the massive amounts of work, he decided that he needed two co-authors to help him write under the pseudonym of "Publius." He originally had asked others to assist him in the project but, luckily for him and future generations, James Madison, a Virginia citizen, was available because the Continental Congress was sitting in New York during that period. John Jay was also asked because of his vast foreign diplomatic service. Unfortunately, John Jay was injured shortly after the project commenced and was able to only complete six different papers. That left Hamilton and Madison to finish the rest, a task they were able to complete only because they relied heavily on notes they had used in the Constitutional Convention in Philadelphia earlier.

Eventually, the books were published serially in different newspapers in New York (four out of five of the major newspapers of the time) as well as republished in book form near the end of the run. Unfortunately, the ratification vote in New York failed and New Yorkers only ratified the constitution after Delaware was the ninth state that approved ratification, which might have rendered New York as a sole state looking in at a union. James Madison, however, took the published books to assist in the ratification debate in Virginia and the papers survived for a far greater purpose than merely propaganda. The Federalist Papers are the single greatest interpretive source of the Constitution of the United States, the best insight and explanation of what the Founding Fathers purpose was in the passage of the document that governs the United States of America.

Philosophically, The Federalist Papers should also be considered in the context in which they were written. The revolutionary era was characterized by a quest for security from foreign nations, for peace in America, and for individual freedom. These values, it was hoped, could be achieved by united action. And whereas earlier plans of union were largely motivated by a desire for security and peace, those of the period under consideration were the first appearance of the freedom motif. That motif came to the fore during the colonists' struggle with England and was recognized by the Articles of Confederation. In the arguments in Philadelphia and the subsequent Federalist Papers this same motif held force and arguments of unity and security, while seeming almost absurd to readers familiar with the power of the modern United States, were sincere concerns and problems.

Major Themes

Energy

A major goal of the proposed constitution was to create a government with sufficient energy to rule effectively. By energy, the authors of the federalist papers essentially mean the power to address national problems and perform the proper functions of government.

Union

The authors of the Federalist papers argue vigorously in defense of the need for a union of all thirteen states. In the early years of American independence, many in America wanted the states to become sovereign countries only loosely connected with one another. The Federalist argues that the liberty of Americans depends on them maintaining their national unity.

Delegated Authority

This is one of the central principles of republican government. Delegated authority refers primarily to the people giving the authority to make and implement laws to elected representatives.

Separation of Powers

A major goal of the Constitution's authors was to ensure that no one branch of government had enough power to become tyrannical and violate the rights and liberties of the people. By distributing power among different branches of government, the founders hoped to prevent one branch from dominating all the others.

Checks and Balances

Closely related to the theme of separation of powers, checks and balances refers to the specific ability of the three branches of government to limit the use of powers by one another. Each branch is granted specific powers over the other two branches, with no one branch able to usurp power from its fellows.

Federal Government

Federal government refers to a separation of powers between a central, national government and inferior political entities. In the US, power and responsibility is shared between state governments and the national government.

Republican Government

The essence of republican government is representation in a legislature. The people elect representatives who then decide on public matters. Republican government was the ideal towards which the founders strove.

Glossary of Terms

Anti-Federalists

Refers to the diverse group of opponents of the proposed US Constitution. Although their specific viewpoints varied, anti-federalists generally favored a weaker central government and stronger state governments.

Articles of Confederation

The original system of government for the United States adopted in 1777. The Articles created a national legislature with broad responsibilities but severely limited capacity to carry out those responsibilities. It quickly became clear that the national government under the Articles was too weak to govern effectively.

Bill of Attainder

A law passed by the legislature that pronounces a person guilty of a crime without first being tried in court.

Canon Law

Laws that govern Christian churches

Charles I

English monarch who was eventually defeated by an army raised by the parliament. Charles was eventually executed. His fall from power was an important step towards the creation of a limited monarchy in England.

Civil Law

Based on the system of laws first administered in the Roman Empire, civil law generally refers to non-criminal court cases. Civil cases are not tried before juries.

Comitia

Ancient Roman popular assemblies. Roman forms of government had a significant influence on the founders of the US Constitution.

Common Law

Rules and principles abased on English customs and practices. Common law is typically unwritten and developed over time through legal decisions by judges.

Consul

Chief magistrate of the ancient Roman republic. The office of the consul influenced the creation of the office of the presidency in the US Constitution

English Bill of Rights

This English political document, adopted in 1689, established the principle of a limited monarchy and the supremacy of Parliament in the United Kingdom.

Ex post facto law

A law criminal created retroactively that punishes the accused for an act which, when committed, was actually legal.

Faction

A group of people with a specific interest or political objective that they are willing to advance at all costs. Faction had a deeply pejorative meaning during the debate over the Constitution.

Federalist

An early supported of the proposed constitution. Federalists generally favored a strong, united central government.

Feudalism

A system of government the centered on the relationship between lord and vassal. The vassal would pledge loyalty to his lord and occasionally serve in his army in return for land and protection.

Glorious Revolution

Political revolution in late 17th century England that destroyed the doctrine of a divine right for rule and established the political supremacy of the parliament.

Habeas Corpus

The legal right of arrested individuals to be brought before a judge to determine whether the arrest is lawful.

Magna Carta

Ancient English political document which established the principal that all Englishmen are entitled to liberty and subject to the law. The Magna Carta is considered to be the foundation of all Anglo-American political liberties.

Oliver Cromwell

English dictator who ruled in the middle of the 17th century. He is referred to throughout the Federalist Papers as a tyrant and serves as an example of the kind of disaster the Constitution was designed to prevent.

Parliament

The English legislature, which serves as the supreme political authority in the United Kingdom. Since America adopted much of its political principles from the English, the nature of the English parliament had a significant influence over the debate in American about the proposed constitution.

Shay's Rebellion

An uprising by farmers in Massachusetts from 1786-1787 in response to economic hardships. Although the rebellion was quelled by the state militia, it caused concern throughout the country that the government under the Articles of Confederation was too weak to maintain law and order. It served as a powerful argument in support of the stronger national government advocated by the federalists.

Short Summary

The Federalist Papers is a treatise on free government in peace and security. It is the outstanding American contribution to the literature on constitutional democracy and federalism, and a classic of Western political thought. It is, by far, the most authoritative text concerning the interpretation of the American Constitution and an insight into the framers' intent.

Although Hamilton carefully outlined the contents of the Federalist papers at the end of the first essay, in reality he strayed a bit from his original proposition. In the end, the work of primarily Madison and Hamilton can be divided into two main parts; the first discussing the defects of the present government, the Articles of Confederation , and the second discussing the new constitutions different components of the legislature, executive, and judicial branches.

The Federalist was written in order to secure the ratification of a constitution providing for a more perfect union. Throughout the papers, the idea of the more perfect union occupies a front stage. On first glance, this might be the primary purpose of the papers but indeed, the Federalist Papers are concerned with much more. "Union" and the "safety and welfare of the parts of which it is composed" are depicted as inseparable, and the Union appears as a means to achieve the safety and welfare of its parts. In general, then, the Federalists discuses federalism as a means to achieve free government in peace and security.

The federalists deal with not only the practical, but also the theoretical, something that distinguishes this from other works. In a letter to his nephew Thomas Mann Randolph, Thomas Jefferson distinguished the Federalist from the theoretical writings of Locke when he writes, after discussing Locke's philosophy: "Descending from theory to practice, there can be no better book than The Federalist." The authors, however, never considered their work a mere treatise on governmental practice. In their essays, a distinction between theory and practice is often drawn. "Theoretical reasoning must be qualified by the lessons of practice," Madison writes, and he also states that the Philadelphia Convention "must have been compelled to sacrifice theoretical prosperity to the force of extraneous consideration."

Five basic themes can be discerned from the words of Hamilton, Madison, and Jay, including federalism, checks and balances, separated powers, pluralism, and representation. Although they deal with different parts of the government, as noted above, these themes are fairly consistent throughout the papers. Much has been written concerning the dual nature of the Federalist Papers, because they were written by multiple authors in a short amount of time. It is true, Madison later became the great state rights' defenders while Hamilton his principle opponent, but for the most part these essays are coherent, showing all sides of the proposed constitution.

Quotes and Analysis

"If these states should either be wholly disunited, or only united in partial confederacies, a man must be far gone in Utopian speculations, who can seriously doubt that the subdivisions into which they might be thrown, would have frequent and violent contests with each other. To presume a want of motives for such contests, as an argument against their existence, would be to forget that men are ambitious, vindictive, and rapacious. To look for a continuation of harmony between a number of independent unconnected sovereignties, situated in the same neighbourhood, would be to disregard the uniform course of human events, and to set at defiance the accumulated experience of ages."

No. 6, page 21

This quote explains one of the core arguments defending the union of the thirteen independent states into a single country under a national government. Hamilton argues here that were the states to be independent and completely sovereign, they would inevitably go to war with one another, just as all other neighboring countries throughout the world have done throughout history. Hamilton frequently dismisses his opponents as indulging in "utopian" fantasies and overly idealistic assessments of human nature when they predict that the states will live together in harmony without a national government over them.

"Among the numerous advantages promised by a well constructed union, none deserves to be more accurately developed, than its tendency to break and control the violence of faction."

No. 10, page 42

One of the core problems facing any political system, according to Madison, is the phenomenon of faction. By faction, Madison refers to any group of people who have a particular interest or ideological point of view. He implies that factions often are willing to sacrifice the public good for the sake of advancing their own position. Madison believes that a united America will be able to avoid the disruptive influence of factions. This is primarily due to the size of the US. The country will be so large that it will be very difficult for a single faction to dominate the political process to the detriment of the union.

"Liberty is to faction, what air is to fire, an aliment, without which it instantly expires. But it could not be a less folly to abolish liberty, which is essential to political life, because it nourish faction, than it would be to wish the annihilation of air, which is essential to animal life, because it imparts to fire its destructive agency."

This is one of the most memorable and widely cited quotes of the Federalist Papers. One option for dealing with faction, according to Madison, would be to simply take away liberty. If people are not free to form and express their own points of view, then factions could never take hold. However, this solution is worse than the problem. Instead, Madison advocates designing a system of government that can control and limit the detrimental effects of faction.

"A nation, despicable by its weakness, forfeits even the privilege of being neutral."

No. 11, Page 51

This quote occurs in the context of one of Hamilton's many papers defending the usefulness of the union. He argues that a united America will be strong enough to field a powerful navy to deter foreign powers from bullying the US. Hamilton feared that a disunited America could easily be overwhelmed by greedy foreign powers.

"It is, that in a democracy, the people meet and exercise the government in person: in a republic, they assemble and administer it by their representatives and agents. A democracy, consequently, must be confined to a small spot. A republic may be extended over a large region."

No. 14, Page 63

Some anti-federalists had argued that America was too large to be governed by a single republican government. However, Madison retorts that the people making this argument have confused democracy, which requires all the people to meet together in person and make decisions on public matters, with republican government, which leaves public matters to be decided on by elected representatives. Since the proposed constitution would create a republican system of government, it could be extended across a country as large as the US. Although it would be impractical for the entire population of the US to gather in a single place to make decisions, it is very possible to have a far smaller number of representatives meet in the capital.

"The great and radical vice, in the construction of the existing confederation, is in the principle of legislation for states or governments, in their corporate or collective capacities, and as contradistinguished from the individuals of whom they consist."

No. 15, page 71

A major criticism of the Articles of Confederation was that it did not give the national government the power to pass laws directly applicable to individual citizens. Instead, laws could only be passed that required certain action from state governments. It is much easier, according to Hamilton, for a state to resist the decrees of the central government than for an individual citizen to do so. As a result, the government under the Articles was weak and ineffectual. Furthermore, the government was fundamentally unstable and constantly at risk of war, since the only way for the national government to enforce its decrees is through the use or threat of violence. If the national government were to resort to force against states, civil war would be the result.

"The idea of restraining the legislative authority, in the means for providing for the national defence, is one of those refinements, which owe their origin to a zeal for liberty more ardent than enlightened."

No. 26, page 127

This quote occurs in the context of Hamilton's defense of Congress's power to raise standing armies under the proposed constitution. Many anti-federalists feared that the congressional ability to raise and maintain armies could lead to tyranny and abuse. However, Hamilton contends that such a viewpoint is unreasonable. No nation can be strong and independent without the means for national defense.

"...but cool and candid people will at once reflect, that the purest of human blessings must have a portion of alloy in them; that the choice must always be made, if not of the lesser evil, at least of the greater, not the perfect good; and that in every political institution, a power to advance the public happiness, involves a discretion which may be misapplied an abused."

No. 41, page 207

This quote, by James Madison, illustrates an important general response to several criticisms levied against the proposed constitution by the anti-federalists. Madison here is calling for political pragmatism and recognition of the fact that no political system can be perfect. The anti-federalists came up with numerous hypothetical scenarios for how the powers granted to the government under the Constitution might be abused. Madison responds to these by saying that any power can be used for good or for evil. The solution cannot be to deny government the power to act in the public interest just because that power might be abused.

"Let the compromising expedient of the constitution be mutually adopted, which regards them as inhabitants, but as debased by servitude below the equal level of free inhabitants, which regards the slave as divested of two-fifths of the man."

No. 54, page 284

This quote, by Madison, illustrates the greatest moral failing of the US Constitution.

It describes the clause in the constitution that stipulated slaves would only be considered three-fifths human for the sake of census taking and determining how many representatives would be apportioned to each state. The phrase "compromising expedient" is key. Clearly, Madison was not comfortable with this clause. It is clear that he felt slavery was an abomination, but, for the sake of preserving the union, he and his allies felt it was necessary to accept this compromise in order to secure the ratification of the Constitution by all the states.

"It is a just observation, that the people commonly intend the public good. This often applies to their very errors. But their good sense would despise the adulator who should pretend, that they always reason right about the means of promoting it."
No. 71, page 370

This quote by Hamilton occurs in the context of his defense of the powers of the presidency outlined in the proposed constitution. Specifically, Hamilton was defending the length of the presidential term as essential to ensuring the executive branch was strong enough to govern effectively. Anti-federalists had been asserting that it was better to have a weak president who could be easily controlled by the people and their representatives in Congress. Hamilton argues however that, although the people's intentions are good, they don't always make the correct policy decisions. They can be influenced by demagogues or "temporary delusion" into making the wrong decision. Therefore, it is critical for the executive to serve as a check on the transient and changing will of the people. It is the role of the president to serve as the national leader and to act wisely in the best interests of the people.

Summary and Analysis of Essay 1

Summary:

Alexander Hamilton begins this brilliant discourse on the Constitution of the United States of America by asking his readers to consider a new Constitution because they have experienced the inefficiencies of the present form of government. He pronounces that the people are in a unique position to answer the most important political question of all: – "whether societies of men are really capable or not of establishing good government from reflection and choice." If the people are up to the challenge, their actions will have great worldwide significance.

He proceeds to show that many people will oppose the Constitution for a variety of reasons, especially if they benefit from the current form of government. Hamilton, however, is not going to address the motives of those who oppose the Constitution; rather, his intent is to make arguments that are for the Constitution. He addresses people questioning his willingness to listen to other arguments because he has already made up his mind to support the Constitution. However, he admits that, while his motives for urging ratification of the Constitution are personal, his arguments are open.

Finally, he outlines the specific issues that he will address in the Federalist Papers, namely, political prosperity and the Constitution; the inadequacy of the present government to preserve the union; the necessity of a strong and energetic government; the Constitution and its relationship to republican principles of government; the similarity of the proposed Constitution to the New York state constitution; and the protection of liberty and property under the proposed government. In addition, he is also attempting to effectively answer serious arguments brought against ratification.

Hamilton concludes the first section of the Federalist Papers by telling the people that it might seem unnecessary to plead for a strong Union, but the country is too large to establish a national system of government. In the end, however, the last question is whether the people adopt the Constitution or whether they will see the end of a united government.

Analysis:

Before beginning a more general analysis of Alexander Hamilton's remarks, it is necessary to provide the background of the political theory of educated men in the United States. First, most educated men, especially those who were at the heart of governing the new country, were extremely familiar with the republics of Ancient Greece and Rome (for example, see John Adam's book *Defense of the Constitution*, published at the same time as The Federalist Papers). From this background, the primary fear was that while a republican government was desirable in order to defend liberty, it was not possible over a large geographic area, such as the United States, because it had never been accomplished before. Rather, this problem had always been the downfall of republics (for instance, the fall of the Roman Empire). The other major pitfall of republics had been class war, something that the Founding Fathers had seen in the recent Shay's Rebellion.

More specifically regarding the text, the introduction to the Federalist Papers contains the outline of Hamilton's "argument," the basic points that he wishes to discuss for ratifying the new Constitution. He also explains his motives and those of his cohorts, explaining that this will not be a debate between two sides of the argument, but rather a coherent examination of the strengths of and necessity for the new Constitution. In this article, therefore, the most important part is the outline Hamilton provides, enabling the reader to classify the remaining 84 papers with ease.

It is also interesting to note that the "world-wide" fame that Hamilton speaks of in this essay occurred, just as the Founding Father predicted. The United States Constitution that Hamilton defended has become one of the most copied and admired documents in the history of civilization. Indeed, the Federalist itself was published in Spanish in 1811 by the Venezualan Manuel Garcia de Sana, along with copies of the Declaration of Independence and the Constitution. In addition, the Federalist influenced movements in Argentina, Mexico, Brazil, and in Europe. Not only did Hamilton's predictions come true, but his very words were influential far beyond the original thirteen colonies.

In summation, after reading Federalist 1, Hamilton, perhaps more than any of the founders, believed in the future greatness of America; he believed that this nation could be one of power and strength, that such power and strength, far from corrupting the nation's purpose or the rights of individuals, alone could bring to realization the former and protect the latter. The very use of the word "empire" in this paper is very telling. Characteristically, he looks ahead; he "dips into the future' and sees the Untied States as a world power. While this might not seem odd to the modern reader, in 1788 America was extremely vulnerable to European conquest and domination, not vice versa. His vision for America is even more remarkable under these circumstances.

Summary and Analysis of Essay 2

Summary:

In one of the few articles written by John Jay, the author begins by stating two facts of political life: some form of government is necessary in a society and all forms of government must be granted sufficient power to regulate conflict and administer the laws. The people grant these powers. For Jay, any establishment of government implies that the people grant the government certain rights that they formerly reserved to only themselves. Given this background, the American people must decide what form of government will best protect their safety and interests. The choice before them is between uniting under one national government or becoming separate states. Clearly Jay believes the first is the better option.

Jay continues that there is no longer a common consensus that America's prosperity depends on being firmly united. At the time of writing, some politicians (with increasing amount of supporters) argued that the country should not have a central government, and should instead exist as separate sovereign states. Jay's aim is to answer this argument. First, he contends that the country is already united in several natural ways. The geography of the beautiful land suggests that we remain a united people because the navigable streams and rivers, which encourage transportation and trade, connect the states. More importantly, he argues that the people worship the same God, come from the same land, speak the same language, have similar manners and customs, and believe in the same principles of government.

For Jay, however, the recently fought Revolutionary War was the main reason to stay united. When the decision was made to form a national government, the states were in a period of crisis.– Jay eloquently describes how, by necessity, the government was hastily formed. Those Articles of Confederation no longer meet the needs of the new country, and given the circumstances surrounding its inception this is not surprising. Jay believes that the United States is fortunate that intelligent men realize the necessity of forming a government now, before rebellions become out of hand. The Constitutional Convention was composed of extraordinary men who deliberated for four months, unwed by power and free from corrupting influences. Their remarkable plan reflects the quality of their deliberations.

Jay concludes that it is significant that this plan is recommended and not imposed. He explains that the framers do not ask for blind acceptance, but rather want sober consideration, equal to the importance of the subject. John Jay concludes by noting that his observation is that the majority of the people are for the new Constitution. Men in their midst who will profit from the separation of the states should not be allowed to "put the continues of the Union in the utmost jeopardy."

Analysis:

In this essay, John Jay deals with general arguments that favor a united nation, rather than breaking up and relying on the sovereignty of individual states. Like many of the Federalist Papers, elements within this essay make it much more than merely propaganda in a newspaper; it is a philosophical work on human nature. As Jay describes the reason that government exists at all and the theory regarding natural rights, he transcends his purpose and makes the work valuable on a philosophical level, and more than a simple defense of the Constitution.

In order to fully comprehend Jay's argument against the desolation of a national government and the sovereignty of states, one must understand the political climate of this period. As the Articles of Confederation were failing, men were not optimistic about the outcome of the fledgling country. Instead, they were asking questions such as: "Had the Revolution been a mistake from the beginning? Had the blood and treasurer of Americans spent in seven years of war against England ironically produced republican systems in which rich and poor New Englanders must engage in bloody warfare against each other? Had Independence merely guaranteed a structure in which Virginians and Pennsylvanian would cut each others throats until one conquered the other or some foreign crown conquered both?"

It was under this fear that the Constitution was developed, and it was with these fears still facing the nation that Hamilton and his partners set out in convincing the nation that the Constitution of the Convention of 1787 was the best possible course for preserving liberty and republicanism in a united nation. His rhetoric concerning the decease of the country, in the conclusion of this essay, therefore, is not merely a scare tactic, as modern readers might interpret, but rather a realistic fear given the political situation in the young country.

It is important to note some of the beliefs and ideals of John Jay, as Federalist #2 is one of the few federalist papers that he wrote (due to sickness, he wrote only 2-5 and 64). Aside from being a strong believer in free government, Jay was a promoter of peace within the United States. As early as 1779, he regretted that Congress, being instituted mainly for the purpose of opposing the tyranny of Britain and for establishing independence, had no authority to interfere in the particular quarrels of the states. Two years later, he continued this philosophy by criticizing the constitution of Massachusetts for describing the state "as being in New England, as well as in America," and wrote "perhaps it would be better if these distinctions were permitted to die away." His biographer relates that Jay even rejoiced that various families were intermarrying with those of other states, because this was conducive to friendship among the states. This essay, therefore, is a natural outgrowth of a long-lived philosophy. Jay was therefore a natural collaborator with Alexander Hamilton.

Summary and Analysis of Essay 3

Summary:

John Jay begins by stating that for a number of years, the general consensus among the people has been that the best government for the nation would be a national government, invested with sufficient power "for all general purposes." He then says that the more that he carefully examines the issues, the more convinced he is that the people are right. For him, the greatest issue concerning government is the safety of the people. In this essay he will argue that a "cordial Union under an efficient national Government, affords the best security that can be devised against hostilities from abroad."

Jay argues that wars are proportional to the just causes to go to war, and so by examining whether a United States would have fewer causes versus the separate states, you can discern which form of government would most likely preserve the peace of the land. Jay then tells his readers that America has already formed treaties with six nations, all of which except for Prussia are maritime nations and could readily injure the United States. It is of paramount importance, therefore, to maintain these relationships with these countries, especially considering the importance they hold to commerce in the young nation. To him, it seems that "one national government" could observe the laws of the nation "more perfectly and punctually" than thirteen separate state governments. First, for Jay, one government has available the "best men of the country," in effect, pooling the best men in each state, city, county, etc and utilizing them for one common cause. Thus, the administration, the counsel, and the judicial decisions will be "more wise" in a united government, and create a "safer" situation for foreign affairs to be conducted. Next, Jay argues that treaties in the national government will be argued and executed in the same manner, not in thirteen different ways. In addition, because each state has different desires and wants, persuasion that is not truly for their common good might influence them more than the nation as a whole; a national government is never subject to making treaties based on local circumstance. Jay also believes that empirical evidence proves his point: by his count, not one Indian war has been provoked by the national government, but several states have provoked such wars, leading to the "slaughter of many innocent inhabitants."

In sum, "not only fewer just causes of war will be given by the national Government, but it will also be more in their power to accommodate and settle them amicably." Jay concludes by citing an example from history. In 1685, Genoa, a small state, offended Louis XIV and was forced to send their chief magistrate and four of their senators to personally apologize and receive his terms. Jay asks: would Spain or Britain or "any other powerful nation" have had to undergo the same humiliation?

Analysis:

All of John Jay's essays for The Federalist Papers deal with the international advantages of adoption of the Constitution. This essay's basic thrust is that the Constitution is necessary in order to make the United States a powerful force, and thus defend her people and their liberties from foreign attacks or domination. Jay's focus can be accounted for simply: Jay had been closely involved in the diplomacy of the Confederation, for which he had acted as ambassador to Spain and as Secretary for Foreign Affairs. Through this work, he knew all the disadvantages to which the Confederation was exposed in foreign relations. It is appropriate that Jay was the author of this specific essay.

Many critics and first time readers of the Federalist Papers argue that Jay had a different agenda and conception of the new Constitution. Jay was not concerned with the same principles of factions and majorities that Hamilton and Madison concern themselves with, critics argue, and Jay was concerned only about making the country powerful enough to deter foreign attacks. This, however, is far from the case.

At first sight, it may appear as if Jay's mention of the people's safety and of their life, liberty, and property, means only that these rights will be guaranteed from foreign attacks. However, consider the politics of the time in which the challenge of individual rights had its origin. Jay was aware of the oppressive majority rule which existed in some of the states. Jay, when pleading for the prosperity of America and the rights of her citizens, recognized the danger arising from the then existing democratic despotism and wanted the individual protected from that quarter as much as from aggressive foreign nations. This is confirmed by him in this federalist paper, when he states that the Union, as established under the constitution, is securing "the preservation of peace and tranquility" not only "against dangers from foreign arms and influence," but also "from dangers of the like kind arising from domestic causes."

There is no reason to believe that Jay conceives of a faction in a different way than his co-authors, who obviously have in mind the infringements upon minority rights under the Articles of Confederation. Jay also complains that "the prospect of present loss or advantage may often tempt the governing party in one or two states to swerve from good faith and justice" and is glad that "those temptations, not reaching the other States, and consequently having little or no influence on the national government, the temptation will be fruitless, and good faith and justice be preserver."

Thus, Jay is not arguing differently, but rather applying the future argument of Madison (for example, in Federalist #10) and Hamilton (Federalist #9) regarding the dangers of factions to the principles of the safety against foreign powers. Jay is as fearful of majoritarianism as his co-authors and merely gives another reason to be fearful of factions: that of defending the country from foreign attack.

Summary and Analysis of Essay 4

Summary

In this paper, John Jay continues his argument in favor of a strong union under a single national government. He contends that such a united government will be better able to deter foreign aggression, particularly from Great Britain, France and Spain. Jay argues that America's growing economic influence as a trading nation creates tension between American and foreign commercial interests. This tension may lead to foreign powers going to war with the United States, even if the United States gave no just cause for war. Jay argues that a single government can better organize a strong and coordinated defense against foreign aggression than an America divided into multiple independent bodies.

Analysis

This paper advances one of the core arguments of the Federalist Papers, which is that uniting the thirteen American states under a single union with significant powers will better serve the people. This paper speaks to what Jay asserts is the primary concern of any people: security.

Jay structures his argument around a single question: which form of government can best defend Americans from foreign aggression? Is it a single national government with strong powers, or multiple independent governments each representing an individual state or loose confederation of states? He puts this question in the context of America's growing commercial influence and the inevitable tensions that will arise from economic competition with European powers.

He then asks his readers to consider whether a united government will be better able to defend against foreign aggression than a disunited government. He uses the example of Great Britain and asks what would happen if its constituent parts (Wales, Scotland, England and Ireland) all had separate militias responsible for national defense. He suggests that if the United States were divided among multiple sovereign governments, then Americans would be less likely to come to one another's aid in a time of war. Foreign aggressors could exploit the disunity within the US and pursue a strategy of divide and conquer.

Summary and Analysis of Essay 5

Summary

John Jay continues his argument against dividing the US into multiple independent sovereign states in this paper. Drawing on examples from British History, Jay argues that if America were divided into three or four nations, it would be constantly beset by jealousies, tensions, disputes and war. He argues that the different American nations would inevitably reach different levels of power and progress. This would lead to envy, fear, and destructive competition.

The different nations would furthermore have different commercial concerns, which would in turn lead to different interests. These differences would likely result in the American nations forming different alliances with foreign powers, culminating perhaps in a situation in which one American nation goes to war with another American nation's ally.

Analysis

In this paper, John Jay is calling on Americans to learn from European history and choose union over disunion. He is responding to anti-federalist arguments that Americans' interests are best served by dividing the country into multiple sovereignties. He contends that such a course of action would produce a weak, fractious America constantly at war with itself.

John Jay is also seeking to use fear of foreign domination to garner support for the concept of a single American union. Essentially, Jay is condensing the array of options facing Americans within a single compelling question: will America allow itself to become weak, divided, and at risk of foreign manipulation, or will it learn the lessons of history and build a strong union under a single national government capable of resisting the European powers?

Summary and Analysis of Essay 6

Summary:

To answer critics that claim the states will prevent conflict between themselves because of the power of commerce, Hamilton says that contrary to belief, it is not in the interest of any nation to be philanthropic with their neighbors.

Republics, just like monarchies, are addicted to war. Both types of government are administered by men, and they can just as easily fall whim to the wants of a few men, just as the republics of Athens, Venice, Holland, and Carthage -- commercial republics all -- likewise fell. Most importantly, Britain, who is extremely active in commerce, has been one of the most warring nations of history. Hamilton also warns against popular wars, such as in the case of Austria, which fought many popular wars based on the idea of commerce.

Hamilton concludes by warning the people to cease to be foolish. The recent events and the depth to which the country has sunk should serve as warning. He then quotes another source, claiming "Neighboring States are naturally enemies of each other."

Analysis:

The basic thrust of this federalist paper, like 6-9, is discussing "the dangers which in all probability flow from the dissensions between the states themselves, and from domestic factions and convulsions." Hamilton believed that if the states remained joined in a mere "partial" confederacy, they would inevitably have "frequent and violent contests with each other." The arguments and historic examples given in this essay mirror not only the Convention speech, but also his argument he had written for The Contientalist in 1781.

One thing that becomes clear in this essay is the Founding Father's desperate fear of the states dividing into separate political entities. Notice that in this essay Hamilton is not arguing against a weaker form of government, or the reinstatement of the Articles of Confederation. Rather his fear was of the dissolution of a country altogether. To modern readers, this fear might seem silly. But in the political climate of the time, without a strong Constitution, the Articles of Confederation would have merely dissolved and the states would have been on their own. His fears, then, however absurd to the reader conscious of the modern superpower and federal government that has made individual states much less powerful than in colonial America, were well-founded.

In future essays, specifically, numbers 18-20, Madison reinforces Hamilton's arguments by an appeal to different historical examples, namely the Amphictonic Council, the Achean League, the Holy Roman Empire, the Swiss Confederation, and the United Netherlands. In writing these essays, Madison, like Hamilton, did not originate new examples, due to the time constraints, but turned to his elaborate research memorandum entitled "notes of Ancient and Modern Confederacies."

It is interesting to compare Madison's careful and scholarly use of history in his essays with Hamilton's, as it reveals clearly the different personal qualities of the two men. The New Yorker, Hamilton, was not scholarly in his approach to politics; his use of history was that of a propagandist citing examples from the past in order to make a debater's point, rather than to establish historical truth. Madison's treatment of Greek confederations was based on widely gathered material from all the available authorities, carefully cross-checked and qualified before being synthesized into a rich study. Hamilton's research consisted in superficially extracting bits of a speech of Demosthenes and a hasty reading of Plutarch.

This is not to say that on topics in which he was interested Hamilton could not write brilliantly and profoundly. On the problem of war treated in this federalist paper, his thought is both mature and suggestive. But Hamilton was not really interested in the problems of federalism, and even on subjects like war and finance to which his mind was congenial his approach was less of the scholar in politics than of the brilliant publicist.

Summary and Analysis of Essay 7

Summary

In this paper, Alexander Hamilton continues his argument for a union over a system of multiple, independent American sovereignties. Hamilton argues that if the American states are not united under a single national government they will have the same inducements to go to war with each other as all other neighboring nations in the world. In particular, he details how territorial disputes, commercial competition, and management of the public debt could all lead to conflicts between the states.

He concludes by arguing that all these sources of conflict would ultimately cause America to be weak, disunited, and at great risk of falling prey to the "artifices and machinations" of foreign powers.

Analysis

In this paper, Hamilton continues his spirited defense of the superiority of the union dictated by the Constitution over his opponent's calls for a system of multiple independent American states. He supports his arguments by creating a series of hypothetical situations in which competing interests between the states could lead to war.

While in his previous paper Hamilton used the divisions of Europe as an example of how easily neighboring nations can be drawn into war, he chooses in this paper to situate his arguments in the context of current events in American society. In so doing, he is making his arguments seem more relevant to his New York audience, who would surely remember the serious tensions surrounding competing territorial claims with its neighbors. He furthermore constructs hypothetical situations in which competing commercial interests between New York and other states could lead to conflict and imagines situations in which different views on the public debt could spark violence.

In essence, Hamilton is attempting in this paper to make more believable his claim that disunion will lead to conflict and instability in America.

Summary and Analysis of Essay 8

Summary:

Hamilton begins this Federalist paper by assuming that he has proven to his readers that the union provides safety from foreign attack, and wants to proceed and address some of the other consequences of the dissolution of the states. Of paramount interest to Hamilton is "war between the states," something this author believes would be "accompanied with much greater distresses than it commonly is in those countries, where regular military establishments have long obtained."

While Europe has many fortifications against military advance, the United States has none. Instead, the United States has a wide-open frontier, and geography that would create a situation where the "populous states would with little difficulty overrun their less populous neighbors." War would consequently be more deadly than in Europe. Because of this fact, standing armies would soon become a necessity and standing armies, regardless of the form of government, "compel nations the most attached to liberty, to resort for repose and security, to institutions, which have a tendency to destroy their civil and political rights."

The weaker states would have the first need of standing armies, an institution Hamilton despises, and would thus, in Hamilton's opinion, make the state governments evolve towards monarchy, because a strong executive is necessary during war. The small states, in Hamilton's suppositions, would have more power over the larger states, and the larger states would result to the same methods of defense that the smaller states first resorted to.

Next, Hamilton distinguishes between countries with military establishments who are frequently subject to invasion, and states that do not deal with this dilemma. A country that is not subject to invasion has no excuse for a standing army, while a country constantly under the threat of an invasion has an excuse for an army. In a country where there is a standing army because of the constant threat of invasion, people's liberties are infringed upon. Great Britain is a country in the first situation. Because of the sea insulating it from attack, the people would never stand for a standing army, and thus, liberty is defended. Hamilton concludes, "if we are wise enough to preserve the union, we may for ages enjoy an advantage similar to that of an insulated situation," thus holding off Europe and her colonies and putting all of the states at the greatest advantage possible.

Analysis:

It is interesting that Hamilton, Madison, and Jay (but most of all Hamilton, as the instigator of this project) chose the safety of the nation as the first topic of discussion in the Federalist Papers. While this subject may seem repetitive and almost absurd to the modern day reader, who reads the Federalist Papers for entirely different reasons, this was the main thrust behind the people's ratification of the Constitution. Reading this paper it becomes clear that this was originally intended as a work of propaganda, not a philosophic discourse.

The main thrust behind this paper is that the United States will prevent internal wars by becoming united as a country, rather than falling apart and battling each other. The analogies between Europe and the United States are interesting to ponder. Hamilton's belief that the United States would only be insulated from war by joining together leaves an analogous question: would Europe have suffered as many deadly wars had they become a united country? While this is impossible to answer because the parallels and opportunities were never provided, as well as the fact that the barrier of language and culture was much more of a problem, it is worth noting as an intellectual consideration.

Notice the reoccurrence of the founding father's reliance on ancient Greece as an example. Although Greece does not fit the paradigm that Hamilton is drawing, he feels it is important enough to note why Greece was an exception. In The Federalist Papers, however, the founding fathers were deliberate –in using experience as their guide. John Adams wrote in 1786, "the History of Greece should be to our countrymen what is called in many families on the Continent, a boudoir, an octagonal apartment in a house, with a full-length mirror on every side, and another in the ceiling. The use of it is, when any of the young ladies, or young gentleman if you will, are at any times a little out of humor, they may retire to a place where in whatever direction they turn their eyes, they see their own faces and figures multiplied without end. By thus beholding their own beautiful persons and seeing, at the same time, the deformity brought upon them by their anger, they may recover their tempers and their charms together." Such was the Founding Father's reverence for the history of Greece, something not duplicated in our own culture.

Summary and Analysis of Essay 9

Summary

Alexander Hamilton explains that "a firm Union will be of the utmost moment to the peace and liberty of the States as a barrier against domestic faction and insurrection." While other republics have provided good examples, they are merely examples and should be used as a starting place, not an ending place. Improvements have been made in political science, as well as the other sciences, since their inception. Hamilton trusts that at some point in history, America's constitution will also be a starting place for governance. These improvements include "balances and checks," such as the elected judges and two separate legislative bodies to represent different aspects of the people. After making these assertions, Hamilton makes an astute analogy, comparing the nation and the states to an orbit of planets around the sun, each still being their own entity but all forced to orbit around something more powerful in order to survive.

Hamilton concludes that the utility of a confederacy is to suppress faction, to guard the internal tranquility of States, and to increase their external force and security. For Hamilton, a strong government would be able to suppress rebellions in other parts of the country because they would not have the same ties to the region - this is an advantage of a larger republic. He believes that people who use Montesquieu's arguments against the size of a nation not being suitable for a republic are false and using the philosopher's words out of context. To try and persuade people that they are wrong, Hamilton quotes the philosopher at length. The majority of Montesquieu's comments used by Hamilton are concerned with the value of the size of a republic in avoiding internal corruption, domestic factions, and insurrections, not the impossibility of liberty existing in a large republic.

The author then proceeds to discuss the difference between a confederacy and a consolidation of States. While people believe a confederation to be an alliance with no "object of internal administration," Hamilton believes this position is arbitrary, with no basis in precedent or principle. For him, the definition of a confederate republic is an "assemblage of societies," or an association of two or more States into one State. The rest is the discretion of those involved in forming the government. As long as there is no abolition of state governments, something that is not proposed by the Constitution, the government is indeed a confederation. Hamilton concludes his essay with an example of the Lycian confederacy, a government that existed with representation based on the size of the population. Montesquieu, speaking of this association, said "were I to give a model of an excellent confederate republic, it would be that of Lycia." Hamilton, then, emphasizes that the novelties in the Constitution are not completely new and even approved by the philosopher most frequently quoted by critics.

Analysis

It is important to understand Alexander Hamilton's political philosophy in order to clearly view this essay. During the Constitutional Convention, Hamilton proposed to copy the British constitution as closely as possible. In the first place, he advocated the creation of a senate that would correspond to the House of Lords and represent the wealthy few. Recognizing the impossibility of making this upper house hereditary, Hamilton nevertheless hoped to give it strength and power by electing senators for life. The chief "organ" of Hamilton's "strong souled" government, however, was not its senate but its elective king. As Hamilton insisted in Philadelphia, nothing less would check "the amazing violence & turbulence of the democratic spirit." This "republican" monarch, like the senate, would be elected for life; he would have power to veto all national legislation, and the prerogative of appointing the governors of all the states, which would thus, under Hamilton's scheme, be reduced to administrative satrapies of the national government. Finally, he hoped this elective king would be given control of the patronage in order to bribe the legislature and insure a steady administration. His study of England had convinced him that this "corruption" was required for a stable government.

This "strong souled" government copied after England's was Hamilton's ideal for America. Only in the establishment of a state which institutionalized in its very organs a "will" independent of the people could the class struggle be allayed in the Untied States. When the Convention turned Hamilton's scheme down in favor of the more democratic and responsible government outlined in the Virginia Plan, he was bitterly disappointed. In July he left the Convention and returned to Philadelphia only for the last sessions. When he signed the Constitution he admitted "no man's ideas were more remote from the plan than his were known to be." He further confessed that this signature was given only because the choice was between "anarchy and Convulsion on one side, and the chance of good to be expected from the plan on the other."

It was in this same spirit of disdain, only partially concealed, that Hamilton wrote as Publius, especially in #9. He was never reconciled to the Constitution's "weakness" as long as he lived. Even while he was preparing to write The Federalist, he drew up a private memorandum in which he prophesied its failure unless additional power could be "squeezed out its clauses by interpretation." Hamilton felt so strongly about the need for an overruling, irresponsible, and unlimited government that it showed through even in his Federalist essays, in spite of his attempt to conceal his opinions in order to achieve ratification. Federalist 9 indicates clearly that he expected a continual use of military force to be necessary for keeping the rebellious poor in their place. In this essay the union is advocated because it will permit the use of troops raised in one section of the country to stamp out revolts in other districts, an expedient restored to Hamilton during the Whiskey Rebellion.

It is characteristic of the different outlooks of Alexander Hamilton and James Madison that Hamilton, in this Federalist Paper, advocated the new union because it will make it easier to suppress with military forces such outbreaks as Shay's Rebellion, while James Madison, in Federalist #10, argues that the union will prevent the recurrence of any such outbreaks. Hamilton prized the union as an instrument guaranteeing that the rich would win every class struggle; Madison hoped that union would prevent class war from being declared in the first place. This dichotomy is part of the internal conflict of the Federalist Papers, something for which many critics have criticized this document. In contrary, these two different approaches provide two different aspects of the constitution, allowing both to become an important part of this philosophic document.

Summary and Analysis of Essay 10

Summary

Madison begins perhaps the most famous of the Federalist papers by stating that one of the strongest arguments in favor of the Constitution is the fact that it establishes a government capable of controlling the violence and damage caused by factions. Madison defines factions as groups of people who gather together to protect and promote their special economic interests and political opinions. Although these factions are at odds with each other, they frequently work against the public interest, and infringe upon the rights of others.

Both supporters and opponents of the plan are concerned with the political instability produced by rival factions. The state governments have not succeeded in solving this problem; in fact, the situation is so problematic that people are disillusioned with all politicians and blame government for their problems. Consequently, a form of popular government that can deal successfully with this problem has a great deal to recommend it.

Given the nature of man, factions are inevitable. As long as men hold different opinions, have different amounts of wealth, and own different amount of property, they will continue to fraternize with people who are most similar to them. Both serious and trivial reasons account for the formation of factions but the most important source of faction is the unequal distribution of property. Men of greater ability and talent tend to possess more property than those of lesser ability, and since the first object of government is to protect and encourage ability, it follows that the rights of property owners must be protected. Property is divided unequally, and, in addition, there are many different kinds of property. and men have different interests depending upon the kind of property they own. For example, the interests of landowners differ from those who own businesses. Government must not only protect the conflicting interests of property owners but must, at the same time, successfully regulate the conflicts between those with and without property.

To Madison, there are only two ways to control a faction: to remove its causes and to control its effects. The first is impossible. There are only two ways to remove the causes of a faction: destroy liberty or give every citizen the same opinions, passions, and interests. Destroying liberty is a "cure worse then the disease itself," and the second is impracticable. The causes of factions are thus part of the nature of man and we must deal with their effects and accept their existence. The government created by the Constitution controls the damage caused by such factions.

The framers established a representative form of government, a government in which the many elect the few who govern. Pure or direct democracies (countries in which all the citizens participate directly in making the laws) cannot possibly control factious conflicts. This is because the strongest and largest faction dominates, and there is no way to protect weak factions against the actions of an obnoxious individual or a strong majority. Direct democracies cannot effectively protect personal and property rights and have always been characterized by conflict.

If the new plan of government is adopted, Madison hopes that the men elected to office will be wise and good men,– the best of America. Theoretically, those who govern should be the least likely to sacrifice the public good to temporary condition, but the opposite might happen. Men who are members of particular factions, or who have prejudices or evil motives might manage, by intrigue or corruption, to win elections and then betray the interests of the people. However, the possibility of this happening in a large country, such as the United States, is greatly reduced. The likelihood that public office will be held by qualified men is greater in large countries because there will be more representatives chosen by a greater number of citizens. This makes it more difficult for the candidates to deceive the people. Representative government is needed in large countries, not to protect the people from the tyranny of the few, but to guard against the rule of the mob.

In large republics, factions will be numerous, but they will be weaker than in small, direct democracies where it is easier for factions to consolidate their strength. In this country, leaders of factions may be able to influence state governments to support unsound economic and political policies –as the states, far from being abolished, retain much of their sovereignty. If the framers had abolished the state governments, the opponents of the proposed government would have a legitimate objection.

The immediate object of the constitution is to bring the present thirteen states into a secure union. Almost every state, old and new, will have one boundary next to territory owned by a foreign nation. The states farthest from the center of the country will be most endangered by these foreign countries; they may find it inconvenient to send representatives long distances to the capitol, but in terms of safety and protection they stand to gain the most from a strong national government.

Madison concludes that he presents these previous arguments because he is confident that many will not listen to those "prophets of gloom" who say that the proposed government is unworkable. For this founding father, it seems incredible that these gloomy voices suggest abandonment of the idea of coming together in strength –- the states still have common interests. Madison concludes that "according to the degree of pleasure and pride we feel in being Republicans, ought to be our zeal in cherishing the spirit and supporting the character of Federalists."

Analysis

James Madison carried to the Convention a plan that was the exact opposite of Hamilton's. In fact, the theory he advocated at Philadelphia and in his Federalist essays was developed as a republican substitute for the New Yorker's "high toned" scheme of state. Madison was convinced that the class struggle would be ameliorated in America by establishing a limited federal government that would make functional use of the vast size of the country and the existence of the states as active political organisms. He argued in his "Notes on Confederacy," in his Convention speeches, and again in Federalist 10 that if an extended republic was set up including a multiplicity of economic, geographic, social, religious, and sectional interests, these interests, by checking each other, would prevent American society from being divided into the clashing armies of the rich and the poor. Thus, if no interstate proletariat could become organized on purely economic lines, the property of the rich would be safe even though the mass of the people held political power. Madison's solution for the class struggle was not to set up an absolute and irresponsible state to regiment society from above; he was never willing to sacrifice liberty to gain security. He wished to multiply the deposits of political power in the state itself sufficiently to break down the sole dualism of rich and poor and thus to guarantee both liberty and security. This, as he stated in Federalist 10, would provide a "republican remedy for the diseases most incident to republican government."

It is also interesting to note that James Madison was the most creative and philosophical disciple of the Scottish school of science and politics in the Philadelphia Convention. His effectiveness as an advocate of a new constitution, and of the particular constitution that was drawn up in Philadelphia in 1787, was certainly based in a large part on his personal experience in public life and his personal knowledge of the conditions of American in 1787. But Madison's greatness as a statesmen rests in part on his ability to set his limited personal experience in the context of the experience of men in other ages and times, thus giving extra insight to his political formulations.

His most amazing political prophecy, contained within the pages of Federalist 10, was that the size of the United States and its variety of interests could be made a guarantee of stability and justice under the new constitution. When Madison made this prophecy, the accepted opinion among all sophisticated politicians was exactly the opposite. It was David Hume's speculations on the "Idea of a Perfect Commonwealth," first published in 1752, that most stimulated James Madison's' thought on factions. In this essay Hume disclaimed any attempt to substitute a political utopia for "the common botched and inaccurate governments which seemed to serve imperfect men so well. Nevertheless, he argued, the idea of a perfect commonwealth "is surely the most worthy curiosity of any the wit of man can possibly devise. And who knows, if this controversy were fixed by the universal consent of the wise and learned, but, in some future age, an opportunity might be afforded of reducing the theory to practice, either by a dissolution of some old government, or by the combination of men to form a new one, in some distant part of the world. " At the end of Hume's essay was a discussion that was of interest to Madison. The Scot casually demolished the Montesquieu small-republic theory; and it was this part of the essay, contained in a single page, that was to serve Madison in new-modeling a "botched" Confederation "in a distant part of the world." Hume said that "in a large government, which is modeled with masterly skill, there is compass and room enough to refine the democracy, from the lower people, who may be admitted into the first elections or first concoction of the commonwealth, to the higher magistrate, who direct all the movements. At the same time, the parts are so distant and remote, that it is very difficult, either by intrigue, prejudice, or passion, to hurry them into any measure against the public interest." Hume's analysis here had turned the small-territory republic theory upside down: if a free state could once be established in a large area, it would be stable and safe from the effects of faction. Madison had found the answer to Montesquieu. He had also found in embryonic form his own theory of the extended federal republic.

In Hume's essay lay the germ for Madison's theory of the extended republic. It is interesting to see how he took these scattered and incomplete fragments and built them into an intellectual and theoretical structure of his own. Madison's first full statement of this hypothesis appeared in his "Notes on the Confederacy" written in April 1787, eight months before the final version of it was published as the tenth Federalist. Starting with the proposition that "in republican Government, the majority, however, composed, ultimately give the law," Madison then asks what is to restrain an interested majority from unjust violations of the minority's rights? Three motives might be claimed to meliorate the selfishness of the majority: first, "prudent regard for their own good, as involved in the general . . . good" second, "respect for character" and finally, religious scruples. After examining each in its turn Madison concludes that they are but a frail bulwark against a ruthless party.

When one examines these two papers in which Hume and Madison summed up the eighteenth century's most profound thought on political parties, it becomes increasingly clear that the young American used the earlier work in preparing a survey on factions through the ages to introduce his own discussion of faction in America. Hume's work was admirably adapted to this purpose. It was philosophical and scientific in the best tradition of the Enlightenment. The facile domination of faction had been a commonplace in English politics for a hundred years, as Whig and Tory vociferously sought to fasten the label on each other. But the Scot, very little interested as a partisan and very much so as a social scientist, treated the subject therefore in psychological, intellectual, and socioeconomic terms. Throughout all history, he discovered, mankind has been divided into factions based either on personal loyalty to some leader or upon some "sentiment or interest" common to the group as a unit. This latter type he called a "Real" as distinguished from the "personal" faction. Finally, he subdivided the "real factions" into parties based on "interest, upon principle," or upon affection."

Hume spent well over five pages dissecting these three types; but Madison, while determined to be inclusive, had not the space to go into such minute analysis. Besides, he was more intent now on developing the cure than on describing the malady. He therefore consolidated Hume's two-page treatment of "personal" factions and his long discussion of parties based on "principle and affection" into a single sentence. The tenth Federalist reads" "A zeal for different opinions concerning religion, concerning government, and many other points, as well of speculation as of practice; an attachment to different leaders ambitiously contending for pre-eminence and power; or to persons of other descriptions whose fortunes have been interesting to the human passions, have, in turn, divided mankind into parties, inflamed them with mutual animosity, and rendered them much more disposed to vex ad oppress each other than to co-operate for their common good." It is hard to conceive of a more perfect example of the concentration of idea and meaning than Madison achieved in this famous sentence.

Summary and Analysis of Essay 11

Summary:

In this paper, Alexander Hamilton continues the defense of union over disunion by outlining the benefits of the former for American commerce and naval power. He argues that in order for Americans to maintain an active commerce, by which he means the ability to control and shape the terms of its trade with foreign powers, America requires a union. He argues that only a union will be strong enough to secure favorable terms of trade with European powers.

He contends further that a united America will be able to pool its diverse resources in building a powerful navy. This navy would then help deter European powers from threatening American commercial interests and stealing American resources. It would furthermore give America significant influence in shaping the international politics of the West Indies where the European powers have significant commercial interests. Hamilton warns that were America to find itself in a state of disunion, the individual states would be too weak to resist the predatory behavior of European powers who would be able to impose unfair terms of trade on the Americans. America would ultimately be reduced to what Hamilton calls a "passive commerce," which would enrich foreign powers at the expense of American merchants.

Analysis

In this paper, Hamilton continues the Federalist's argument in defense of union and a vigorous national government by exploring the consequences of union or disunion for American commerce and Naval power. These arguments were particularly compelling to the Federalist's New York audience, since that state was one of the most active centers of commerce on the continent at that time. Although Hamilton focuses on the commercial and naval implications of the proposed form of government, this paper basically advances a very similar argument outlined in previous papers: a union will bring strength and enable America to resist foreign aggression, whereas a disunited America will be subject to European bullying.

Hamilton furthermore invokes the adventurous spirit of Americans, who are, Hamilton implies, inherently commercial in their outlook. To a significant extent, Hamilton is seeking to convince his audience to support the Constitution by appealing to their financial interests. New Yorkers should support the Constitution because only a united America can protect their ability to enjoy favorable terms of trade.

However, Hamilton takes this argument beyond purely pecuniary interests by portraying Europeans as arrogantly subjecting the peoples of Asia, Africa, and America to domination and economic exploitation. He draws on the notion of American exceptionalism and calls on his countrymen "to vindicate the honor of the human race" by standing up to European predation. He concludes by warning that, were Americans to become disunited, they would become just another victim of European imperialism.

Summary and Analysis of Essay 12

Summary

In this paper, Hamilton continues his defense of the union provided for by the Constitution by arguing that a single national government will be better able to collect taxes than individual, disunited states. He bases his argument on the assertions that a steady source of revenue is essential to the strength of any nation and that taxes on commerce and consumption are more desirable then direct taxes on individuals based on what they produce. He contends that if America were divided into multiple states or confederacies, it would be very easy for smugglers to bypass the commercial taxes put in place by the various states.

He uses the example of France's difficulty in patrolling its large land border with neighboring European countries and contends that smugglers could use the many land borders between the states to avoid tax collectors. For example, if New York had higher taxes than New Jersey, an English merchant could bring his goods to a New Jersey port, smuggle them across the border to New York and thus avoid the higher New York taxes. If, however, America were united as a single country, it would only need to patrol its Atlantic sea border and would thus be able to better secure taxes from foreign trade. Hamilton warns that if America is disunited then commercial taxes will soon prove insufficient, forcing the states to levy oppressive taxes on land owners.

Analysis

This paper builds on the previous paper's argument that a union will promote American commerce and foreign trade. It argues that not only will a union encourage prosperous trade but it will also enable the government to collect large amounts of revenue from that trade. This revenue will then serve as the foundation of power of the American government. This paper furthers one of the core arguments of the Federalist Papers: a union will be strong and prosperous while a system of independent states will be weak and ineffectual.

Hamilton furthermore seeks to play on the fears of American property owners that they will be burdened with excessive taxes on their land if commercial sources of revenue prove inadequate. Hamilton warns that when state governments inevitably discover that they cannot collect sufficient revenue from commerce due to uncontrollable smuggling, they will be forced to rely on taxing Americans directly.

Summary and Analysis of Essay 13

Summary

In this short paper, Hamilton argues that a union will be more cost effective than a system of multiple American sovereignties. If America were to be divided into thirteen independent states, or some smaller number of confederacies, each polity would have to employ its own "civil list," or bureaucracy, to manage public affairs. Each state would furthermore have to employ people to guard its borders against illicit trade and an army to defend against invasion. All these expenses would prove to be a significant and unnecessary burden to each sovereignty's economy.

In contrast, united America would be able to make do with a single national government, a single army, and a single entity responsible for catching smugglers. This would reduce waste and inefficiency. Hamilton points to the example of Great Britain's government to argue that a single, well-structured, national government could easily be extended to cover large swaths of territory and big populations.

Analysis

This short paper is essentially an addendum to Hamilton's previous arguments outlining the economic benefits of union over disunion. Hamilton is essentially arguing that an America united under a single national government would have a much more efficient government and economy. If America were divided into multiple independent countries, each country would have to employ its own bureaucrats, an expense Hamilton dismisses as wasteful and unnecessary.

This paper illustrates the central tension in the American system of government between efficiency and liberty. Anti-federalists were animated by the fear of a distant, all-powerful central government that would suppress the rights of the people by force. They believed that by locating political authority at the local and state level, Americans would be better able to keep their political leaders in check and prevent them from amassing sufficient power to establish a tyranny. However, Hamilton argues that the massive inefficiency and bureaucratic excess created by so many independent states would have the net effect of overburdening local economies. Government costs money and, therefore, having more governments with more power would lead to exorbitant administrative costs.

Summary and Analysis of Essay 14

Summary

In this paper, Madison seeks to counter the arguments made by opponents of the Constitution that America is too large a country to be governed as a united republic. He argues that these critics, in arguing that a republic must be confined to a small territory, have confused a republic with a democracy. The difference, according to Madison, is that in a democracy the people meet and exercise the government in person, whereas in a republic the people govern the country through their elected representatives. Because a republic has representatives, it can extend over a large region. Madison calculates in some detail the size of the United States and argues that it is not too large to be governed by a republic, especially when compared to Great Britain and other European countries.

Madison argues further that the general government will only be authorized to deal with issues of concern to the entire republic. State governments will be left to deal with local concerns, thus making the administration of a country as vast as the US more manageable. Furthermore, as America becomes more developed with roads, canals and other infrastructure, it will be easier for the states to communicate and thus easier for the national government to administer the country. Finally, although representatives from those states farthest from the capitol (such as Georgia) will have longer to travel, they will also be in greater need of the benefits of union due to the dangers inherent in being a frontier.

Madison concludes this paper by exhorting Americans not to destroy their unity. He dismisses those who say no country has ever succeeded in what Americans are trying to accomplish, and encourages Americans to boldly accomplish what has not been accomplished before.

Analysis

In this paper, Madison brings to a close the opening section of the Federalist Papers defending the benefits of union over disunion. The previous papers having established the benefits of union, Madison now seeks to address unanswered objections brought against the creation of a united system of American states under a single national government. He begins the paper by methodically answering each objection in a highly rational, measured and detailed argument.

However, having laid out the facts, Madison appeals to Americans' sense of exceptionalism and spirit of individualism. He argues that Americans are distinguished by their willingness to trust their own good sense rather than be controlled by "a blind veneration for antiquity." He describes Americans as courageous innovators willing to take risks and become an example for all mankind to follow. By taking this approach, Madison seeks to rouse American passions. He is not only speaking to their heads, but appealing to their patriotism as well.

Summary and Analysis of Essay 15

Summary

Hamilton begins by telling the people that in the previous papers he has tried to convince them of the importance of the Union to "political safety and happiness." In this essay, he changes the theme to the "insufficiency of the present confederation to the preservation of the union." He argues that the majority of the people agree that the present form of government will eventually lead to "impending anarchy." He continues that the United States has reached the "last stage of national humiliation," because of large debts, territories in the possession of a foreign power, a lack of military, a lack of money, inability to navigate on the Mississippi River, lack of commerce, lack of respect by foreign powers, decrease in value of property, and unavailability of credit.

In sum, because of "national disorder, poverty, and insignificance." Hamilton urges that the country must firmly stand for safety, tranquility, dignity, and reputation. He attacks the supporters of the Articles of Confederation, claiming that though they admit that the government is destitute of energy, they stand against "conferring upon it those powers which are requisite to supply that energy," wanting instead, something that is impossible, the augmentation of federal powers without decreasing the powers of the states.

To Hamilton, the biggest problem in the existing government is the principle of legislation for states in a collective manner, which creates multiple sovereigns. Under this situation, the laws of the nation, though constitutionally binding, become merely suggestions that the states can choose to follow or not follow. While he sees nothing wrong with compacts between states, like such treaties that exist throughout the world, from experience he believes that little dependence can be placed on such agreements. He believes that the states of the country could stand in similar relation to each other, and it would not be ideal but would be "consistent and practicable." But if there is still some desire for a national government, it must take on different characteristics from a league of governments: we must extend "the authority of the union to the persons of the citizens, the only proper objects of government." The very idea of a government implies the power of making laws and those laws must contain a consequence, a penalty, applied by the military or the court. Because no system exists under the Articles of Confederation that properly carries out the law (no national court system), the government is useless.

For Hamilton, government was created because the passions of men do not conform to the "dictates of reason and justice" and groups of men act with greater intelligence than individuals alone. Hamilton supposes that this is because reputation has a less active influence.

In addition, he believes that because of the nature of sovereign power, people become obsessed with their own power. A meeting of many sovereign powers, then, like the Articles of Confederation, creates problems because a love of power means that people fail to compromise. The business of the government, therefore, cannot be carried out under this system and national interests become subservient to individual desires and wishes.

Alexander Hamilton, finally, specifically attacks the Articles of Confederation as failing because the system was destined to fail. It did not happen all at once, but instead, gradually, progressing to the point that things have become a "stand-all," with everyone "yielding to the persuasive voice of immediate interest and convenience, till the frail and tottering edifice seems ready to fall upon our heads and to crush us beneath its ruins."

Analysis

In this essay, Hamilton theoretically examines the flaws of a national government that contains multiple sovereigns. During the majority of the essay, (after outlining problems of the United States), he does not attack the Articles of Confederation specifically; instead, he generally laments the basic problems with a particular type of system of government that contains multiple sovereigns, and then, only at the end of the paper, states that the problems are not based on the Articles of Confederation, but any form of government that has this philosophical basis. In later papers (16-22), Hamilton will examine more specifically the many problems that plague the present form of government. In this essay, however, he lays the philosophical problems of the type of government - he must start over completely before he attacks the specific problems of the country.

Both Madison and Hamilton were convinced that local sovereignty had to be abolished, something that they were much more open about in their private correspondence than in their more political public statements. Neither Hamilton nor Madison wanted to see the sates absorbed entirely into a national government, but neither thought that that was likely. It seemed inconceivable to them that a central authority could or would want to descend to enforcement of local laws.

It has to be recognized that the Constitution and the Articles of Confederation allocated power and wealth differently, and hence some groups would be hurt and others benefited by a change in the regime. The arguments used against the Article of Confederation, in many people's opinion, while a classic in political theory were not the primary influence in the ratification of the new Constitution. Instead, as some critics argue, opposition to the proposed Constitution came from those groups whose economic and political position within the state would be threatened by the new order, not by those who opposed it ideologically. The Federalists won so decisively because of agenda control. For example, the Federalists made sure that the states strongly in favor voted first, while they delayed votes in those states where the people were opposed.

Summary and Analysis of Essay 16

Summary

Hamilton begins this essay by restating that it is an absolute fact that the present confederation, because of the manner in which it has been set up, is the "parent of anarchy," and that the delinquencies of the states of the Union are the "natural offspring" that will lead the country to civil war. From this point, Hamilton proceeds to hypothetically go through the consequences of a lack of a large, standing, national army. In Hamilton's opinion, the end would be a war between the states because the strongest state is likely to prevail in any disagreement with no national army to put the states in their proper place. This would be the violent death of the confederacy. The other alternative would the "natural death" - what Hamilton thought the country was in the midst of at the writing of the Federalist Papers. If there is not war between the sates, the states would simply do their own bidding, disregarding the federal government, and the federal government's power would erode until it was completely eradicated.

At this point, Hamilton reminds his reader that the country should prefer a national constitution, and one that has provisions for a large army, "continuously on foot to execute the ordinary requisitions or decrees of the government." While some of the critics of the constitution want to believe that there is an alternative, anything else is impractical. From this argument for a standing army, Hamilton proceeds to discuss the necessity of not governing merely the states, but of the government having power over the individual. The government must "carry its agency to the persons of the citizens." Hamilton proceeds to argue that the individual state legislatures should not have to approve the laws because they could disregard the laws, and their disregard would ruin the system of law in the country. Unity of the country is paramount, and the only way unity can occur is through a strong, national government. Alexander Hamilton concludes his essay by claiming that no government can always avoid or control those who will be disorderly, but it would be "vain to hope to guard against events too mighty for human foresight or precaution, and it would be idle to object to a government because it could not perform impossibilities."

Analysis

This essay continues Alexander Hamilton's theme of the importance of the government to the unity of the country. While this is apparent from the conclusion of the essay, how does the first part of the essay fit with the second part? A standing, national army represents the nation's right to enforce the laws on all of it's citizens. Only by having power over the individual do you have the right to arrest them, to imprison them, and to set them free. This same right also lets the government avoid having to deal with the individual agendas of the differing states. In essence, you bypass their concerns and create a more national government which, in Hamilton's terms, is able to effectively preserve the "general tranquility."

This essay belongs to the second major division of The Federalist, the commentary on "the insufficiency of the present Confederation to the preservation of the Union." While Hamilton wrote 15, 16, and 17, Madison, however, was to write three of the essays of this section, for his careful research on the subject made him more competent than Hamilton to compare the "vices" of the Confederation with the weaknesses of other historic confederacies. Thus, after Hamilton's Federalist 15, 16, and 17 developed the theme that no national government could endure unless it had jurisdiction over the individuals in the states rather than over the states in their corporate capacities, Madison took up his pen again. In Number 18, 19, and 20, he enforced Hamilton's arguments by an appeal to the history of the Amphictyonic Council, the Achaean League, the Holy Roman Empire, the Swiss Confederation, and the United Netherlands. Madison in writing thee essays merely had to turn to his elaborate research memorandum entitled, "Notes of Ancient and Modern Confederacies."

It is interesting to note that Hamilton's conviction regarding peace within the states was not a new-found philosophy, but rather a long-standing belief. During the Revolutionary war, he feared dissensions among the members of the Confederation. Stating that the republics of the Greek leagues as well as the Swiss cantons were continually at war with each other in spite of the vicinity of foreign powers, Hamilton warned that the danger of interstate tensions was considerably greater in America, due to the absence of strong neighbors. He was concerned about disputes over state boundaries, and regretted that the prospects of future tranquility were not flattering. In "The Continentals," published in 1782, Hamilton again reproached the states for their mutual jealousy. When he congratulated Washington at the conclusion of the preliminaries of peace, he added a note of caution, saying that "the centrifugal is much stronger than the centripetal force in these States – the seeds of disunion much more numerous than those of union." He remained concerned about the harmony among states throughout his entire life.

Summary and Analysis of Essay 17

Summary

Hamilton seeks to address concerns that the proposed Constitution will lead to tyranny at the hands of a power-hungry national government. He argues that it is unlikely that men in national office would even be interested in usurping the powers from the states, which relate to concerns that "can never be desirable cares" of a general government.

However, Hamilton argues that even if the national government were to try and usurp power from the states, it would be very difficult for it to do so. He contends that state governments will likely have far more influence over and support from the people then the national government. Essentially, Hamilton is arguing that since states deal with issues that more directly impact the day-to-day lives of the people, especially criminal and civil justice issues, they are more likely to inspire feelings of attachment from the people than a distant, national government would.

As evidence, Hamilton points to European feudal societies and notes that it was very difficult for the sovereign to control his feudal baronies. Hamilton asserts that state governments in the American confederacy are analogous to these feudal baronies in that both are able to effectively resist central control. If anything, Hamilton warns, Americans should be concerned about a federal system leading to anarchy, not tyranny.

Analysis

Hamilton continues to make the case that the present system of government in America, the Articles of Confederation, provides too weak a central government. He is addressing one of the core fears of post-revolution America: that a strong central government will quickly turn into the kind of monarchical system the country fought to escape. Hamilton's argument is based on the belief that human affections are, by nature, "weak in proportion to the distance or diffusiveness of the object." That is, the further away a governmental organization is, the more difficult it will be for that organization to secure the support of the people. Hamilton uses Europe's feudal history, which was characterized by weak central governments, to make the case that federal systems are more likely to lead to anarchy than tyranny.

What is particularly notable about this paper is that Hamilton is using one of the core political beliefs of the anti-federalists against them. The anti-federalists believed that state governments ought to be given significant powers, since they can be most trusted to serve the interests of the people and protect their liberties. The anti-federalists believed that the national government under the proposed constitution would pose a threat to the people and overpower the states. However, Hamilton bases his response on a professed faith in the enduring strength and influence of state governments. His argument implies that the states are indeed, as the anti-federalists believed, guardians of the rights of the people. He argues that, therefore, Americans have nothing to fear from a powerful central government since they will always have the state governments to stand up for their rights.

Summary and Analysis of Essay 18

Summary

In this paper, Madison continues to outline the inadequacies of the Articles of Consideration. His core concern in this paper is to establish the fundamental weaknesses inherent in a system of government composed of multiple sovereigns under a relatively powerless central government.

Madison uses the example of the ancient Greek republics under the Amphyctionic council as historical evidence for why the Articles of Confederation would ultimately lead to disaster in America. He begins by showing that the system of government in this confederation seems to provide the central, governing council with all the powers it would need to keep the confederation strong and prosperous. However, it has a fatal flaw: each republic in the confederation "retained the character of independent and sovereign states, and had equal votes in the federal council." Without an unquestioned higher authority to keep all the constituent republics in check, the council was soon torn apart by various divisions as the more powerful members sought to intimidate and exploit the weaker ones. Ultimately the republics, unable to maintain their unity, fell under the control of foreign powers.

Madison also invokes the example of the Achaean League and suggests that the general authority and laws of the confederacy were able to temper the disorders within the members of the league. By giving up their sovereignty to the confederation, the members of this league experienced fewer disturbances and divisions. The downfall of the league only came when the Achaeans practiced "arts of division" and allowed their union to be dissolved.

Analysis

This paper is essentially an furtherance of the previous paper's argument that federal systems, in which power is shared between a central government and smaller, constituent government, are more likely to suffer from disunity and anarchy than tyranny. This paper is an attempt to directly contradict the argument of anti-federalists that the proposed constitution will lead to the reestablishment of monarchical rule in America.

Madison is furthermore trying to strengthen The Federalist's position on this issue by drawing on examples from Greek history. He is essentially arguing that if Americans do not do away with the Articles of Confederation in favor of a system of government with a stronger national government, the country will ultimately repeat the tragic mistakes of the ancient Greeks.

Summary and Analysis of Essay 19

Summary

Paper 19 is very similar to paper 18. In paper 19, Madison seeks to bolster his argument in favor of a stronger national government by drawing on examples of existing confederacies that have suffered tremendously as a result of inadequate authority being granted to the central government. He points to Germany and, to a lesser extent, Poland as prime examples of what happens when a country lacks strong central control. He points to the violence and instability that marked Germany's feudal system and asserts that the "principal vassals" who constituted the German empire during that period were too powerful to be controlled by the emperor. The result was anarchy.

In the period during which Madison writes, Germany has adopted a federal system that in many respects resembles the American Articles of Confederation. However, the German system, Madison writes, has led to weak and ineffectual governments since the empire is fundamentally "a community of sovereigns." As a result, the emperor is unable to efficiently and reliably control his empire. The empire is consistently beset by civil war and, in the face of foreign aggression, woefully unable to organize a united defense. Germany's neighbors routinely take advantage of the empire's weakness and even pursue a "policy of perpetuating its anarchy and weakness."

Analysis

Madison employs extensive historical evidence to strengthen his position that having a strong, national government with supreme authority over constituent governments is necessary for the long-term strength and stability of any federal system. The example of Germany that Madison uses in this paper would have been familiar to his readers. In comparing the Articles of Confederation to the historically weak and ineffectual German imperial system, Madison provides his readers with a recognizable and memorable illustration of the perils of weak central authority.

In addition to the examples Madison cites here, there are numerous examples from the 21st century of what can happen in a state that lacks sufficiently strong central authority. The east African nation of Somalia has not had a strong, widely recognized central government since the early 1990s. Since then, the country has been beset by numerous civil wars, droughts, famines, and terror attacks. The fundamental problem in Somalia is that no political actor has sufficient power to impose the rule of law over the entire nation. As a result, numerous small militias, tribes and warlords attempt to fill the power vacuum. This leads to endless violence and suffering for the Somali people. Afghanistan, the Democratic Republic of the Congo, and many other "failed states" serve as reminders of what happens when there is no central authority in a state.

Summary and Analysis of Essay 20

Summary

In this paper, Madison continues the theme of the previous several papers that unions composed of co-equal or sovereign states ultimately end in weakness, ineffectual government, civil war, and foreign predation. Madison discusses the United Netherlands, which he describes as a confederacy of aristocracies. He details the extension authorities granted to the central governing body, called the states-general, but then contends that this confederacy is marked by "imbecility in the government; discord among the provinces; foreign influences and indignities; a precarious existence in peace, and peculiar calamities from war." The cause of the Netherlands' troubles, Madison contends, is a system based on "a sovereignty over sovereigns, a government over government, a legislation for communities, as contradistinguished from individuals."

Madison shows that having a weak and "defective constitution" like the Netherlands' can actually lead to tyranny when the central government is pressured to go beyond its constitutional authority in order to respond to crises. In the name of public safety, a central government may simply go beyond the powers allotted to it by a weak and ineffectual constitution.

Analysis

Paper 20 brings to a conclusion the extended argument, begun in paper 15, that the Articles of Confederation do not afford enough power and authority to the national government. The system of government provided for in the Articles ultimately amounts to collection of independent, sovereign states, loosely united under a weak central government. The central government is unable to impose laws directly on the citizens and can only require action from the states. As a result, these paper argue, violence and the "coercion of the sword" inevitably replace law and "coercion of the magistracy." In a system composed of multiple sovereigns, the only way to compel one of those entities to act is through violence. The national government cannot bring a state to court as it can an individual. This is ultimately a recipe for instability, division and civil war.

What the authors of these papers are calling for is a system that allows the national government to create laws that are directly applicable to individual citizens. The national government must have supreme authority. Otherwise, disunion and even anarchy will result from multiple sovereigns (i.e. the thirteen states) competing with one another for supremacy.

Summary and Analysis of Essay 21

Summary

In paper 21, Hamilton builds off of the previous papers' criticism of confederacies that afford too little authority and power to the central government. It discusses three specific issues that illustrate how America's system of government under the Articles has left the national government weak and ineffectual. Hamilton first discusses the inability of the national government to enforce its legislation. The government can pass laws, but it cannot enforce them. States can simply disregard the laws without facing any serious repercussions from the national government.

The second issue relates to what Hamilton calls "a mutual guarantee of the state governments." That is, the national government has no authority to protect state governments from being violently overthrown or torn apart by internal divisions. For example, if a small faction or powerful individual were to forcibly take control of Pennsylvania, the national government under the Articles would have no authority to intervene and restore freedom and justice.

The third issue Hamilton discusses is the inability of the national government to raise revenue from the states. The national government would routinely demand that states contribute certain sums of money to pay for pressing national expenses. However, the government had no way to actually compel states to pay the amount they owe. Hamilton argues that there is no way to fairly calculate how much each state should pay to the national government. He argues that the national government should be able to impose a national consumption tax that all citizens pay directly to the national government. He contends that a consumption tax is the safest tax since, were the government to impose too high a tax, people would simply consume less and thus pay less in taxes. This, Hamilton argues, will keep the tax rate at a reasonable and manageable level.

Analysis

Hamilton is moving beyond a more general discussion of the weaknesses of confederate government into the specific failings of the Articles of Confederation. In the previous several papers, Hamilton and Madison made clear that confederacies marked by weak central governments have repeatedly descended into ineffectualness and anarchy throughout history. Now, Hamilton is showing in very specific terms how the Articles have already started America down that path. The national government cannot enforce its own laws, guarantee the democratic character of state government, or even raise its own revenue.

During the debate over the Constitution, most Americans agreed that the Articles of Confederation had many serious deficiencies that needed to be addressed. According to the authors of the Federalist Papers, one of the most severe failings of the Articles was their failure to provide the central government with "energy." In discussions of the constitutional politics, "energy" refers to the ability of a central government to exercise its authority and impose its will. If a government can only pass laws or make declarations without actually being able to enforce those declarations, then it lacks "energy" and is nothing more than a distant talking-head.

Another striking aspect of this paper for the contemporary American is Hamilton's support for a consumption tax, which is essentially the same as the present-day sales tax. Many economists and some politicians advocate the adoption of a national sales tax in America that would replace most other taxes, including the federal income tax. Hamilton defends the consumption tax by pointing out that Americans will have a very simple way of avoiding the tax: limit consumption. Theoretically, if the government were to raise consumption taxes too high, Americans would simply purchase less, leading to a decline in economic activity and government revenue that would cause the government to reconsider its tax policy.

Summary and Analysis of Essay 22

Summary

Hamilton begins this essay by saying that in addition to the problems of the Article of Confederation that have already been discussed, there are others of equal importance that also need to be addressed.

First, both Federalists and anti-Federalists agree that the lack of power to regulate commerce among the several states and between this government and foreign nations has created an abominable situation. For Hamilton, this is the biggest problem, which motivates a stronger form of government. Foreign governments are understandably reluctant to enter into trade agreements or treaties with us knowing that the individual states can (and do) violate, at their whim, the terms of these agreements. Under these circumstances, the United States cannot develop a favorable balance of trade or enjoy diplomatic relationships. In addition, the lack of uniform trade regulation has resulted in considerable animosity among the states. It is of the utmost importance that the national government have the power to regulate commerce.

Next, Hamilton addresses the subject of the military, a power that under the confederation was merely "making requisitions upon the States for quotas of men." During the Revolution, this system was found wanting because it created competition between the states, "an auction for men." Several states promised their male citizens more money than other states were paying, and men, in attempt to force their states to increase military pay, delayed enlisting. This competition among the states, a type of blackmail, created dangerous situations, including confusion, expense, inefficiency, and undisciplined troops. Nothing but the "enthusiasm of liberty induced the people to endure." Besides the difficulties this situation created, it also was unfair because the states closest to the center of the war inevitably made the largest effort to meet their quotas; those farthest away from the fighting made little or no effort to meet them.

Another issue that Hamilton feels necessitates the new constitution is "the right of equal suffrage among the states." Under the Articles of Confederation, all the states, whether large or small, were represented equally in the Congress. This system, however, means that in reality the people are unequally represented. New Hampshire, Rhode Island, New Jersey, Delaware, Georgia, South Carolina, and Maryland constitute a majority of the states, but they do not contain one-third of the population. Thus, this situation violates the republican principles of majority rule. The citizens of the small states must realize that, sooner or later, the citizens of the large states will protest such an unfair arrangement. When that happens, the stability and welfare of the country will be threatened. A situation in which a responsible majority is frequently coerced by a small minority could result in anarchy. The other problem that arises from this legislative situation (a national government controlled by a legislative minority) is that the government is vulnerable to foreign influence and corruption. It is difficult for a foreign government to influence a governing majority but relatively easy for them to corrupt or influence a powerful few.

The other defect that Hamilton feels is severe is the lack of a Supreme Court, a body necessary to define and interpret the laws, as "laws are dead letter without courts to expound and define their true meaning and operation." In addition, a Supreme Court is needed to interpret and enforce the terms of treaties. A court is given more importance in the United States where laws can conflict. A government cannot exist if local biases and narrow interests dominate the national discourse.

Last, Hamilton attacks the ratification of the Articles of Confederation. Because the Articles of Confederation were ratified by the state legislatures, Hamilton argues that they lack power and could be dismissed easily. Instead, he believes that "the fabric of American Empire ought to rest on the solid basis of the consent of the people."

Analysis

The entirety of this federalist paper, like that of federalist papers 1-22, is devoted not to promoting the new constitution, but to examining the flaws in the existing Articles of Confederation. When this was originally published, on Saturday, December 15, 1787, it marked the completion of the second formal section of the work. Hamilton focuses on five basic themes, all falling under the theme of the strength of federalism, in an attempt to convince the general public of the inadequacies of the present type of government. These themes include the problems dealing with commerce, military, courts, representation, and the ratification of the Articles of Confederation.

Differences and similarities between Alexander Hamilton and James Madison can be gleaned from this paper written by Hamilton. Like Madison, Hamilton believed that democratic excesses in these states threatened the individual's rights. Hamilton wants free government secured through a federal guarantee of the state constitutions. Unlike Madison, Hamilton fears that factions in one state may cause trouble in other states rather than being absorbed and neutralized. Therefore, as later papers demonstrate, Hamilton believes in the concentration of power in the national government. Above all, this article emphasizes the need for "an entire change" of the "radically vicious and unsound" system of the Articles of Confederation.

Interestingly, there were extreme difficulties of penning the Federalist in the short amount of time necessary before the New York ratifying convention met. Luckily, before he even began penning the papers, Hamilton had worked out a detailed outline of a substantial percentage of the essays he had contracted to write for The Federalist. The first two topics to be discussed by Publius were "The utility of the Union" and "The insufficiency of the present Confederation." Hamilton had covered exactly those subjects in the opening pages of a speech delivered at the Constitution Convention. Hamilton, therefore, had a quantity of material recently used at Philadelphia that was presented again, like this essay. Hamilton used the same ideas, theories, and historical examples that he had already used in the convention, thus facilitating the rapid publication of the first essays.

Summary and Analysis of Essay 23

Summary

The the topic of this Federalist paper, authored by Alexander Hamilton, is the "necessity of a Constitution, at least equally energetic with the one proposed, to the preservation of the Union." He outlines three main points:

1) what the Federal Government should provide

2) the amount of power necessary to carry out their positions

3) who in the government should do this

The third point, however, will be discussed later. To Hamilton, the answer to the first question is that the principal purpose of the Union is the common defense of the members, the preservation of public peace, the regulation of commerce, and the conducting of foreign affairs. In order to create a common defense, you have to be able to raise armies, to build and equip fleets, and to create rules for the government of both. Hamilton believed that these powers should exist without limitation because it is impossible to foresee future emergencies. To Hamilton, the means justify the ends in this case of a strong military.

Hamilton believes that even the Articles of Confederation recognized the importance of the military, because there were provisions for Congress to make unlimited requisition of men and money to direct their operations. These requests failed because the states did not have any binding interest. This failure shows us that "we must extend the laws of the federal government to the individual citizens of America." In sum, "the Union ought to be invested with full power to levy troops; to build and equip fleets, and to raise the revenues which will be required for the formation and support of an arm and navy, in the customary and ordinary modes practiced in other governments."

Hamilton continues that the government must have the power to "pass all laws and make all regulation" which pertain to the common safety of the union. If people argue that these powers should not be given to the federal government, Hamilton believes they are sorely mistaken. "A government, the Constitution of which renders it unfit to be trusted with all the powers, which a free people ought to delegate to any government, would be an unsafe and improper depository of the national interests," a situation that the Articles of Confederation have created. Hamilton concludes, that it must be fixed.

Analysis

While many of the Federalist Papers seem repetitive, emphasizing the same points over and over again, it is important to remember that the Federalist Papers were not designed to be like a book, read cover to cover. The papers were individual pieces of propaganda appearing serialized in a newspaper. Clearly, Hamilton, Jay, and Madison did not assume that their readers were familiar with all of their words and hence the repetitive nature of their work.

The "precious advantage" that the United States had in 1787 that offered hope for a "republican remedy for the diseases most incident to republican government" lay in the predominance of small freehold farmers among the American population. Since the time of Aristotle, it had been recognized that yeoman farmers -– a middle class between the greedy rich and the envious poor -– provided the most stable foundation upon which to erect a popular government. This factor, commented on by Madison, Pinckney, Adams, and others, helps explain why the Convention did not feel it necessary to sacrifice either majority rule or popular responsibility in their new Constitution.

It is interesting to note that the plan Hamilton defends in this paper was not theoretically the soundest. The leaders of the Convention realized that a theoretical best –- and member after member went on record praising the British constitution as the best ever created by man –- might be the enemy of a possible good. As Pierce Butler insisted, in a different context, "The people will not bear such innovations. Supposing such an establishment to be useful, we must not venture on it. We must follow the example of Solon who gave the Athenians not the best government he could devise, but the best they would receive."

Summary and Analysis of Essay 24

Summary

In this paper, Hamilton responds to the criticism that the proposed constitution does not have sufficient provisions against the existence of standing armies in times of peace. He does not deny that the constitution allows for the existence of standing armies in peacetime; however, he argues that the critics have left out the fact that the power to raise armies lies in the legislature, not the executive, and that there is little precedent in the state constitutions for prohibiting such forces. Since the power to raise armies lies with the legislature, the people do not need to fear that the government will use the army to violate their rights. Hamilton notes that the army's budget must be approved at least every two years, which he says will help protect against the rise of an excessively powerful military establishment.

Finally, Hamilton argues that the discretion of the legislature to raise armies must not be restrained. He outlines the military threat posed by Spain, Britain, and the Native Americans, and contends that militias will be insufficient to counter them. Even in peacetime, it is necessary to guard the frontiers of the republic and protect seaports. Militias would not be ideal for this function since the volunteer, citizen-soldier militiamen would likely be unwilling to form "that most disagreeable duty" for extended periods of time, and taking militiamen away from their regular jobs would significantly increase expenses.

Analysis

This is the first in a series of papers that seek to address one of the most compelling criticisms of the proposed constitution: that it allowed for the creation of powerful standing armies which would constitute a fundamental threat to American liberty. There is a long tradition of anti-militarism in Anglo-American political thought. British and American political philosophers typically understood standing armies, i.e., professional fighting forces maintained even during peacetime, as instruments of tyranny. In monarchical systems with a strong executive, the sovereign could employ soldiers to impose his will on the people and deprive citizens of their basic rights.

Militias were seen as far safer sources of security since they were populated by the people themselves. Militiamen had regular jobs as farmers, laborers, craftsmen, merchants, etc. They simply trained periodically and fought during crises. In peacetime, they went back to their regular jobs. Militias were seen as inherently republican. Rather than entrusting the nation's security to a band of professional fighters separated from the daily life and economy of the public, individual citizens were responsible for protecting their and their neighbors' property and liberty.

Hamilton seeks to allay these concerns by assuring his readers that standing armies in America will be controlled by the people themselves through their elected representatives in the legislature. Furthermore, he contends that having a standing army is simply unavoidable given the security environment in which America found itself in the late 18th century. He adopts a somewhat mocking tone in addressing his critics and implies that they are exaggerating the risks posed by a standing army in order to stoke the traditional Anglo-American fear of military establishments.

Summary and Analysis of Essay 25

Summary

In this paper, Hamilton continues to defend the Constitution's provision authorizing the legislature to raise armies in times of peace. He first dismisses the proposal offered by opponents of the Constitution to entrust individual states with the responsibility of raising armies under the direction of the national government. He argues that the dangers facing America are common to all states and therefore ought to be dealt with by "common councils" and "a common treasury." He argues that without a nationally controlled standing army, some states would end up bearing a greater share of the defense burden then others. Even more concerning, individual state armies would tempt state governments to use military force to resolve disputes with neighboring states and undermine the national authority.

Hamilton argues further that a national standing army would pose less of a threat to liberty than state armies since the people will be naturally more suspicious of the distant national government than the state governments. He asserts that "the people are commonly most in danger, when the means of injuring their rights are in the possession of those whom they entertain the least suspicion."

Hamilton also asks whether the critics are demanding congress be prohibited from raising armies in times of peace or simply from "keeping them up," i.e., funding an army already established. He argues that if Congress were prohibited from keeping up these forces, it would be unclear what constitutes "keeping them up." Such ambiguity, Hamilton argues, could create an opportunity for the executive and the legislature to elude "the force of the provision" altogether. If, in order to prevent this, Congress were prohibited from raising armies in times of peace, then America would "exhibit the most extraordinary spectacle," a country prohibited from preparing its defense until the enemy had already attacked.

Hamilton argues further that the militias, which train only part-time, will not provide adequate defense against professional armies: "War, like most other things, is a science to be acquired and perfected by diligence, by perseverance, by time, and by practice." Hamilton uses examples of domestic strife in Pennsylvania and Massachusetts as evidence of the need for armies in times of peace to stand ready to quell domestic insurrections and foreign aggression at a moment's notice.

Hamilton closes by arguing that standing armies are an absolute necessity. All societies inevitability look to them in times of danger to provide for public safety. If the American Constitution does not allow for such forces, they will still be created: "…how unequal are parchment provisions, to a struggle with public necessity." These violations in the name of the necessity, however, will undermine the respect which politicians afford to the constitution, creating "a precedent for other breaches."

Analysis

Hamilton's primary goal in this paper is to convince his New York audience of the necessity of granting the national legislature authority to raise and maintain armies during peacetime. He places New York in the category of states that are likely to be most directly exposed to foreign aggression—and thus one of the states in greatest need of protection by a standing army. Hamilton recalls several themes and arguments introduced in previous papers and uses them here in defense of the constitution's provisions for standing armies. Specifically, he warns that multiple state armies will be lead to tensions and even war between the individual states and the unequal sharing of the burden of national defense.

One must be careful not to mistake Hamilton's arguments here as a defense of standing armies in and of themselves. He does not deny that they are dangerous to liberty, but instead argues that they are unavoidable necessities and asserts that the proposed constitution contains sufficient provisions for keeping such national forces in check.

Hamilton's argument here is rooted in a realists' interpretation of national defense. In the wake of the Revolutionary War, in which citizen-soldiers played a pivotal role, Americans had idealistic notions of militias as supreme guardians of republican virtue and national defense. Hamilton, however, contends that in the modern era, professional armies are a necessity.

Hamilton furthermore introduces the notion of the reverence for the Constitution in this paper. He fears that if the document does not provide for standing armies, necessity will nevertheless lead to their creation. Such a violation of the fundamental laws of the country could, Hamilton fears, lead to a diminishing of the esteem with which those laws are held. This would make it easier for politicians down the road to violate the constitution again, even when not circumstances do not necessitate such violations.

Summary and Analysis of Essay 26

Summary

In this paper, Hamilton continues his defense of the proposed constitution's provisions for standing armies in times of peace. He argues that his critics are motivated by a "zeal for liberty more ardent than enlightened," and insists that the nation must adopt a political system that affords government the power it needs to govern while also protecting private rights. He points out that most state constitutions recognize that "confidence must be placed somewhere." That is, although Americans fear an excessively powerful government, it would be far more dangerous to put so many restrictions on the legislative authority that the government cannot do its job.

Hamilton traces American fear of standing armies to the country's British ancestry. Over the course of British history there were numerous examples of kings using armies to enforce absolute rule. It took many generations for the British to limit the power of the monarch and deny him sole control over the military. The Americans have taken this traditional British wariness of standing armies too far, however, and placed too many restrictions on their elected representatives under the Articles of Confederation.

In the proposed constitution, Hamilton argues, the legislature will be required to debate funding for the military every two years. This will ensure that the military never gets too powerful to overthrow American liberties. Two years is too short for the military to acquire overwhelming force and become an instrument of tyranny.

Hamilton concludes by repeating the necessity of having an army. He admits that there will always be some risk of the military becoming a force for tyranny, especially if war necessitates the creation of a very large and powerful military. However, the alternative of lacking an army to defend against foreign aggression and domestic insurrection would be even worse.

Analysis

This paper illustrates one of the central themes of the Constitution: a balance between the "energy" of government and the rights of the people. Armies were traditionally viewed as a threat to the liberties of a people. Professional soldiers, it was feared, could be used by the executive to oppress a lightly armed, inadequately trained population. However, at the same time, armies are necessary to protect the nation.

Hamilton asserts that the constitution adequately balances these competing concerns. It allows for a standing army to be created and maintained, but places the authority for such an action in the hands of the legislature and not the executive. By taking this approach, the constitution balances the necessity of having a standing army with the moral imperative of protecting the rights of the people.

Summary and Analysis of Essay 27

Summary

In this paper, Hamilton addresses concerns that the Constitution will lead ultimately to reliance on military force to implement its laws and decrees. Hamilton argues instead that the federal government will be well-administered by highly competent individuals and that, as a result, it will enjoy the support and willing compliance of the people: "I believe it may be laid down as a general rule, that [the people's] confidence in, and their obedience to, a government, will commonly be proportioned to the goodness or badness of its administration." Furthermore, having a strong federal government will discourage sedition since factions will be less willing to take on the entire force of the union than the power of a single state. If the federal government is given authority to create laws applicable directly to the people, instead of only to the states as collective entities, a strong connection will be built between the citizens and their national government. This will increase the authority of the union and strengthen "the affections of the citizens towards it," so that force will not be necessary for implementing federal laws.

The Articles of Confederation have created a situation in which violent force is the only way for the national government to enforce its laws on the states. Since the states are essentially independent sovereignties, they cannot be compelled to follow national government decrees by means of the judiciary the way an individual citizen could. In contrast, the proposed constitution will provide stability and peace by incorporating all the various state governments within a single national system in which the "laws of the confederacy" are the supreme law of the land.

Analysis

This paper draws on the idea, introduced in previous papers, that a national government with the authority to impose laws on the citizens themselves will ultimately provide for greater stability and peace than a system of independent states loosely connected within a confederation.

Hamilton tries to dismiss the widespread fear of tyrannical government imposing its laws violently by arguing that the people will willingly obey the laws of the federal government. Even if some break the law, such instances can be dealt with through the courts. In contrast, under a system of loosely connected states, the national government would only be able to enforce its laws violently. Thus, in defending the constitution, Hamilton is not denying the validity of its opponents' fears but asserting that the constitution is the country's best bet to prevent these fears from being realized.

Summary and Analysis of Essay 28

Summary

In this paper, Hamilton acknowledges that there may be times in which the government must use force to maintain law and order. However, he contends that this is an unavoidable possibility in any political system. He argues that having a standing army, as opposed to just a militia, will be necessary at times to subdue large scale domestic insurrections or foreign aggression.

Hamilton emphasizes that the people need not fear the military establishment because it will be controlled by a government run by the representatives of the people. However, if for some reason, the representatives of the people were to betray their constituents, the people would be better able to resist "the usurpation of the national rulers" than "those of the rulers of an individual state." If the national government were to use standing armies to usurp power, the people could rally around the state governments and resist the national rulers. The larger the polity, the harder it is for a government to gain absolute control.

In the system designed by the proposed constitution, the state governments would act as natural checks on the national government and vice versa: "power being almost always the rival of power." However, if each state were totally independent and no national army existed, then state governments could more easily violate the rights of the people, who would have very limited means for organizing a strong resistance.

Analysis

In this paper, Hamilton is describing a hypothetical worst-case scenario. Although it may seem unthinkable in 21st century America, the Americans of the 18th century were deeply concerned about an excessively powerful national government using the military to oppress the people. Hamilton is arguing that not only is a national military at times necessary to ensure public safety, but, even were this military to become an instrument of tyranny, the state governments would act as natural centers of resistance.

Hamilton frequently takes the approach of acknowledging a widespread fear among the population—e.g., the fear of violent usurpation of political liberties—and then using a hypothetical situation to illustrate how the proposed constitution offers the best protection against that fear. However, Hamilton also buttresses his hypothetical with current events in order to make his arguments more plausible to his audience. In this paper, he refers to New York state's claim to certain sections of Vermont to illustrate that, although militias can deal with small local issues, they will not be sufficient to deal with major conflicts.

Summary and Analysis of Essay 29

Summary

Hamilton address criticisms of the constitution's provisions for federal control of the militia. Specifically, the constitution empowers the union "to provide for organizing, arming and disciplining the militia, and for governing such part of them as may be employed in the service of the United States, reserving the states respectively the appointment of the officers, and the authority of training the militia according to the discipline prescribed by congress." Hamilton defends this provision by stating that it will reduce the need for large standing armies, which were widely viewed as a threat to liberty.

He furthermore rejects the criticism that the authors of the constitution intended to create a system in which military force would be the primary instrument for enforcing legislation. The critics based their claim on the fact that the constitution lacks any provision for magistrates employing the use of the posse comitatus, which is the authority of a magistrate to enlist the services of able-bodied men to assist him in enforcing the law. Essentially, the critics are claiming that by not specifically authorizing posse comitatus, the constitution is setting up a system under which the government would have to resort to military forces to execute its duties rather than relying the citizens themselves. However, Hamilton points out that the authority granted to congress to "pass all laws necessary and proper to execute its declared powers" would include the authority to require citizens to help officers enforce the law.

Hamilton also suggests how the national government may choose to regulate the militia. He suggests that most militiamen would only muster once a year to ensure that they are properly armed and equipped. In addition there would be a select force that would be more highly trained and stand ready to quickly take to the field whenever the defense of the state required it.

Hamilton furthermore dismisses the claim that granting the federal government authority over state militias would lead to the government using these militias as instruments of tyranny. In particular, critics claimed that one state militia would be used to oppress the people of a different state. Hamilton argues that state militias would never be willing to do such a thing and would instead overthrow the tyrants who issued such orders. Furthermore, the states would retain the right to appoint the officers of the militia, which would guard against them becoming instruments of tyranny.

Finally, Hamilton asserts that federal control over the militia would allow the national government to deploy state militias to different states in times of war. If the national government did not have the authority to do this, then some states might end up bearing a disproportionately high burden during wartime.

Analysis

This paper brings to a close several papers discussing the role of military forces under the proposed constitution. Hamilton's tone in this paper is highly combative and exhibits a high degree of frustration with what he believes to be the unreasonable criticisms of the constitution's opponents. He essentially accuses the critics of disingenuous fear-mongering devoid of all common sense. He sees the fear of a federally controlled militia as particularly absurd since the militia would be composed of "our sons, our brothers, our neighbors, our fellow citizens...". In refuting these counterarguments, Hamilton methodically talks through how the constitutional provisions for the militia would likely play out in the years to follow. He appeals to readers' common sense in arguing that the citizen-soldiers who constitute militias would never willingly become an instrument of tyranny.

This relates to a very important and influential belief of 18th century Americans: militiamen are more trustworthy than active-duty soldiers. It was widely believed in the early years of the republic that full-time soldiers in standing armies were generally of low moral character. They devote their life to fighting and will do anything for money. By contrast, militiamen were believed to be a direct extension of the citizenry into the realm of military activity. Militias were seen as a direct reflection of the people themselves fighting for their own rights and freedom. Serving in the militia was perhaps the highest form of civic virtue. Hamilton draws on this faith in the civic virtue of militias to convince his readers that just because the federal government has some authority over them does not mean that militiamen will suddenly lose their moral character and become the means by which an ambitious politician establishes his autocratic rule.

Summary and Analysis of Essay 30

Summary

In this paper, Hamilton defends the constitution's provisions authorizing the national government to impose taxes on the people directly. Under the Articles of Confederation, Congress could only request funds from the states. Although the states were legally obligated to submit the funds, they often failed to do so, leaving the national government, according to Hamilton, unable to govern effectively.

Hamilton argues that the national government must have sufficient resources to govern the country. He further warns that if the national government cannot raise revenue in a reliable fashion, then the national credit will suffer, since lenders will not trust the US government to pay back its loans. Unable to borrow money in times of crisis, especially wartime, the government would be unable to protect the interests of the United States.

Analysis

This paper fits within one the broader theme of the Federalist Papers: the need for the national government to have sufficient powers, or energy, to govern effectively. In this paper, Hamilton is applying this concept to the topic of taxation. As in other papers, Hamilton illustrates a hypothetical nightmare situation in which the government, at a time of national crisis, is unable to raise sufficient funds to defend the nation. As evidence, Hamilton points to the recent history of the US in which states routinely refused to contribute funds to the national government.

The anti-federalists were very concerned about granting the federal government authority to impose taxes directly on the people. They feared that such authority would enable the federal government to burden the people with oppressive and unreasonable taxes. In fact, throughout American history, many politicians and organizations have equated the power to tax with the power to oppress. Without money, people cannot purchase life essentials, let alone participate actively in society. Theoretically, the government could impose such a high tax burden that the people must spend all their time working just to fulfill their tax obligations. This would leave them with few opportunities to participate in public life and advocate for change. Similarly, locating all the financial resources of the state in the government is akin to making the government all-powerful.

However, Hamilton contends that in order for government to be effective, it must have revenue. He does not deny that granting the federal government the power to tax runs the risk of that power later being abused. However, other papers demonstrate how the proposed constitution will impose checks on the power of the government and ensure that tyrannical government is never established in America.

Summary and Analysis of Essay 31

Summary

Hamilton defends the authority of the federal government to impose taxes "in the ordinary modes," as opposed to taxing the states in their collective capacities, with reference to three principles. First, a government ought to have enough power to fulfill its responsibilities. Second, since it is impossible to predict what problems the US government will face in the future, its ability to confront these challenges must not be unduly limited. Third, since all governments require money to fulfill their responsibilities, it must be granted the ability to generate revenue.

Hamilton furthermore dismisses the conspiracy theories of the constitution's opponents who allege that granting the government the authority to tax the people directly will enable the national government to become tyrannical and leave state governments at "the mercy of the national legislature." Hamilton argues that the structure and composition of the government, rather than the excessive limitation of its powers, must be relied upon to guard against such usurpations.

Analysis

Hamilton prefaces his argument in this paper with a discussion of "primary truths, or first principles." He asserts that certain principles in the natural science are plainly evident. Similarly, in ethics and politics, certain principles are simply common sense. However, in morals and politics, men can easily become stubborn and intractable. He accuses opponents of the Constitution of being unreasonable in their criticisms and argues why the Constitution's provisions for taxation are based on common sense principles of political science. He explicitly recognizes the counterargument that taxation may lead to usurpations of state rights by the national government, but then derides this position as unreasonable and extravagant fantasy.

By taking this approach, Hamilton tries to present his side of the argument as irrefutable and rooted in common sense. His tone is highly argumentative and dismissive. He clearly considers his opponents' arguments to be founded on unreasonable fears that serve only to prolong and confuse the debate.

Summary and Analysis of Essay 32

Summary

This paper discusses the powers of the states and the federal government to impose taxes on the people. It discusses the notion of concurrent powers and exclusive powers as they relate to taxation. Concurrent powers are those that both the states and federal government share. Exclusive powers are those that only the states or the federal government can exercise.

In the case of taxes, the authority of the federal government to levy taxes does not preclude the state governments from doing the same thing since taxation is a concurrent power. The only restriction on the authority of the state governments to levy taxes relates to duties on imports and exports. Congress can levy such taxes, but state governments can only do so with the consent of Congress.

Hamilton acknowledges that the concurrent power of taxation could lead to situations in which state governments and the national government impose taxes on the same item, a situation that might be "inexpedient." However, Hamilton asserts that the prudence of governments can be relied on to avoid such situations. It is not necessarily a "direct contradiction of power" for a state government and Congress to impose the same tax.

Analysis

Hamilton assuages the fear that granting the national government the ability to levy taxes will preclude the states from doing the same thing. Opponents of the constitution feared that if only the federal government could generate revenue, the state government would be left in a severely weakened position.

By protecting the authority of states to impose taxes directly on their inhabitants, the constitution ensures that states remain relevant and effective. This paper illustrates the founders' attempt to balance power between state and federal government.

Summary and Analysis of Essay 33

Summary

Hamilton defends Article 1, Section 8, Clause 18 of the Constitution granting Congress authority to make all laws which shall be necessary and proper for carrying out its powers, and Article 6, Clause 2 which declares national law the supreme law of the land. Opponents of the constitution claimed that these clauses granted too much power to the national government.

Hamilton responds that both clauses are common-sense provisions necessary for any functioning government. If Congress is entrusted with certain tasks, such as raising taxes and maintaining an Army, it must be allowed to do what is "necessary and proper" to fulfill those tasks. Having a power implies being able to do what is necessary to use that power.

Similarly, the very nature of law implies supremacy: "A law, by the very meaning of the term, includes supremacy. It is a rule, which those to whom it is prescribed are bound to observe." If the national government did not have the power to enact binding legislation, then the states would essentially be bound together by treaty rather than government.

Hamilton asserts that granting this authority to the national government does not allow it to enact laws that violate the constitution. Rather, it merely enables it to perform the basic functions of any government. If the national government were to enact a law that violates the rights of the states—such as deny them the ability to levy taxes—then that law could be justly resisted and the national government held accountable by the people for attempting an usurpation of their rights.

Analysis

This paper is another attempt by Hamilton to assuage the fears of Americans that a strong national government would threaten the rights of states and individual citizens. He appeals to his audience's common sense and reminds them that a government must have the ability to pass binding legislation on citizens. Without this authority, a government is not truly a government. He addresses the specific concern of state rights enthusiasts that the federal government might use its power to pass binding legislation in order to take away the ability of states to levy taxes by pointing out that such an action would be unconstitutional and, therefore, not binding.

The "necessary and proper" clause is one of the most important and most controversial clauses in the Constitution. It has been the subject of numerous Supreme Court cases, and has been central to debates throughout American history over the proper role of Congress. Perhaps the central reason for all the debate is the inherent ambiguity in the phrase "necessary and proper." After all, who decides what is "necessary and proper"? Nevertheless, the founders felt that such ambiguity was essential to creating an effective system of government. The founders recognized that they could not predict the numerous complicated issues that America would face in the future. Therefore, they felt compelled to make clear that Congress had the authority to do what was needed in order to perform the proper function of government.

Summary and Analysis of Essay 34

Summary

Hamilton returns to the concept of co-equal authority, or concurrent powers, shared by the state and national governments. He defends the constitution's provision for such powers, particularly as they relate to taxation. He argues that the national government's power to tax must not be limited, since it is impossible to know what will be required by future crises and challenges. Hamilton asserts that wars and rebellions will inevitably threaten the US just as they do every other country. Therefore, the national government must have wide powers to tax the people in order to have sufficient funds to provide for the nation's defense.

Hamilton contends that the concurrent power to tax will not be a problem since the needs of the states will be relatively limited. If the constitution were to limit what the national government can tax in order to secure greater taxation powers for the states, as some opponents of the constitution advocated, then that "would have amounted to a sacrifice of the great interests of the union to the power of the individual states."

Analysis

Hamilton again tries to present his side of the argument as most in tune with reality. He presents his arguments as dispassionate assessments of human nature and the course of human history and portrays his opponents has basing their arguments on unjustifiable fears and the vain hope that human beings can be trusted to do the right thing. He argues that America will face tough times ahead and that the national government must therefore have the power to raise sufficient resources to protect the national interest.

Once again, Hamilton is trying to convince Americans of the necessity of having an energetic government; that is, a government with adequate powers to discharge its duties effectively. He is trying to overcome the widely held suspicion of strong central power and convince Americans of the necessity of reducing the power of the states in favor of the union.

Summary and Analysis of Essay 35

Summary

Hamilton defends the unfettered ability of the national government to levy taxes from the perspective of equality and fairness. He asserts that if the union were only allowed to levy certain taxes, then the tax burden would be unequally distributed among the population. For example, if only imports could be taxed, then merchant classes and states that rely primarily on imports would suffer disproportionately.

Hamilton also answers the claim that the constitution ought to ensure that the house of representatives have representatives from all classes of people, such laborers, merchants, learned professionals, etc. Hamilton responds that such a provision is unnecessary since people from certain classes can still represent those from other classes. For example, merchants have an interest in protecting the interests of manufacturers since they provide the items that merchants trade. Hamilton predicts that the house will mostly be composed of landholders, merchants, and learned professionals (such as lawyers); however, this will not be a problem, since these classes of men are still accountable to voters of all classes and will therefore be motivated to understand their constituents' diverse needs.

Analysis

Hamilton plays on the particular fears of New York voters, whose livelihoods depend heavily on commerce. He warns that restricting the powers of the union to tax only certain items would ultimately lead to an unequal distribution of the tax burden. Hamilton uses the example of an import tax, which would fall disproportionately on states like New York that depend heavily on imports for economic growth.

Hamilton furthermore engages in an interesting discussion on class relations in the United States. Hamilton advances the hypothesis that it is not necessary for the Constitution to impose class-based quotas on the membership of the House of Representatives. He argues essentially that economic and political interests transcend social class. For example, a merchant has an interest in protecting the interests of manufacturers. It is important to note that while this is a widely held view in America's meritocratic society and market-based economy, other civilizations have throughout history adopted very different perspectives. In particular, the 19th and 20th centuries saw the rise of Marxism, which contends that classes have distinct and irreconcilable economic interests.

Summary and Analysis of Essay 36

Summary

Hamilton responds to further criticisms of the constitution's tax provisions. He rejects the claim that the national legislature will not have sufficient knowledge of local circumstances to impose taxes on the people directly. Representatives of each state will certainly have an adequate understanding of their constituent's interests and circumstances in order to make an informed decision on taxation.

Hamilton also addresses concerns about how the national tax system would operate, especially when both states governments and the union have the authority to levy taxes. He asserts that both levels of government would be wise enough to avoid taxing items already taxed by the other. He also asserts that the national legislature will be able to use the state's tax collecting apparatus to collect federal taxes. Finally, Hamilton argues that the proposed constitution will not lead to "double sets of revenue officers" or "double taxations" as had been feared.

Analysis

This paper brings to a close the Federalist's section in defense of the proposed constitution's provisions for taxation. Hamilton addresses lingering fears and specific criticisms that had arisen regarding tax issues in very clear terms. He furthermore offers details on how tax collection would actually work in practice.

Most importantly, Hamilton closes the paper by recalling the central theme of "energy," and reminding voters that in order for a government to be effective, it must have sufficient revenue. Life in America under the Articles had shown the futility of expecting states to reliably and consistently contribute funds to the national government. It was essential, according to Hamilton, that the national government have extensive powers to raise revenue directly without the interference of the states.

Summary and Analysis of Essay 37

Summary

In order to convince the readers that a government must be at least as energetic and strong as the one proposed, they must carefully examine the defects of the existing government. Madison does not expect people to accept the merits of the Constitution on faith alone. By examining the provisions of the constitution and comparing each provision, Madison will attempt to calculate the effects of the new government on the nation and its citizens.

For Madison, it is one of the ironies of human affairs that important public matters are seldom examined objectively. A new plan of government excites passion and prejudices, not surprisingly. The founding fathers believed those who opposed the Constitution only briefly looked at its contents. But some who write in favor of the Constitution are guilty of the same and much of their supportive writing lacks substance and critical analysis.

There is, however, one critical difference between the supporters and critics of the Constitution: those who support the Constitution superficially usually do so because they know the existing government is weak and the country is in a serious situation: a forgivable fault. The critics, however, cannot be forgiven. But Madison is not writing to either of the two biased groups. Instead, this paper is written for those who sincerely are in favor of and want to promote the welfare of the country and who will listen to reasonable arguments and explanations. In order to appreciate the proposed government, you have to realize that no plan is faultless. The Convention, like all groups, was composed of fallible men. Fallible men drafted the Constitution and fallible men in the end will judge it.

Madison argues that the readers must not only accept the fallibility of men, but also try to understand the difficult task the framers faced. What was done in Philadelphia had no precedent. The framers began their deliberations knowing that the structure of government was weak because the underlying principles that governed it were unsound. They realized that they could not erect a strong structure upon a weak foundation. Unfortunately, the principles to build the Constitution were hard to find because the framers could not look to other confederacies because they, too, were founded on unsound principles. Studying both ancient and modern confederacies served only to warn them of what should be avoided in the establishment of the new government. As a result, the framers took as their "textbook" the experience of this and other countries, not political theories.

One of the most important and difficult problems was how to establish an energetic and stable government without threatening the liberties of the people. Had the framers not solved this problem, they would have failed. Stability in government promotes confidence and is essential to national character. Stability is threatened if too many people hold power, and energetic government requires that the execution of the laws should be the responsibility of one man, the president. But in a free society power is derived from the people and those who hold office are responsible to them. The proposed government reconciles and balances these two important values. Stability is achieved through the principle of representation; liberty is protected because the government rests upon the consent of the people. In addition, a part of this balance was achieved by establishing relatively short terms of office for representatives, senators, and the president.

Another problem the framers faced was how best to divide authority and power between the state and national governments, something that was extremely difficult. The framers also had to wrestle with the problem of describing in specific detail the purpose and limits of different codes of laws and types of courts. The English studied this problem for years, but never came up with specific solutions. No language supplies words and phrases for every complex idea or is so precise that every word has only one meaning. The Convention also faced other problems. The delegates had to reconcile the conflict and competition between the large and small states, as well as the fact that competing sectional interests had to be reconciled, as did various economic and social conflicts within every state. These competing interests will undoubtedly have a beneficial effect on the proposed government, but to reconcile them during the Convention was a difficult task.

Madison concludes that it is remarkable given all of the pressures and difficulties that an agreement was reached at all. While it is easy for a theorist to plan a perfect document in the privacy of his den or imagination, for men to hammer out their differences together is another matter. Madison attributes two factors to the success of the Constitutional Convention: first, the framers were free of party animosities and second, the delegates were so pleased with the final product that they were willing to put aside certain personal objections in order to avoid further delay or the necessity of drafting an entirely new document.

Analysis

Federalist Number 37 is the beginning of another of James Madison's series of work. Hamilton's series of fourteen papers on the vital need for an energetic constitution ended with Number 36, published on January 8, 1788. On January 11, Madison commenced with 37, explaining how the Convention had combined "energy in government with the inviolable attention due to liberty and to the republican form." In this division of the work so peculiarly suited to his talent he had occasion not only to develop the federal principles of the Constitution, but also to discuss in his own characteristic vein the various questions that lie at the foundation of free government itself. And although twelve of the twenty-four essays he wrote in this section have been claimed by Hamilton, examinations of the papers themselves show they were indubitably written by Madison.

Madison's' first two essays, not only 37 but also 38, were devoted to the difficulties faced by the Convention in guaranteeing both the security of the few and the liberty of the many. Madison's thoughts on the relationship of liberty and authority are interesting, because this is a problem that had been his chief concern since he had entered politics. He eloquently wrote in Federalist 37, "Energy in government is essential to that security against external and internal danger and to that prompt and salutary execution of the law, which enter into the very definition of good government. Stability in government is essential to national character. . . On comparing, however, these valuable ingredients with the vital principles of liberty, we must perceive at once the difficulty of mingling them in their due proportions."

While Madison complains in this Federalist paper that the founding fathers had no guides, this is not completely true as they relied heavily upon the philosophers of their time and of earlier times. Raynal, Delome, Montesquieu, and Hume, are, among others, expressly mentioned and quoted within the Federalist Papers themselves, but these writers do not exhaust the list of those whose impact on the Papers is obvious. Machiavelli, and Hume; Hobbes and Rousseau; Harrington, Coke and Clackston, and above all Locke, were all intellectual forebears of the Federalist's discussion of constitutional democracy. While some of theses authors were fundamentally accepted by Madison, Hamilton, and Jay, others were probably fundamentally rejected. No one philosophy was taken over completely or, for that matter, completely rejected.

It is probably no exaggeration, however, to say that Locke exercised a greater influence upon American political thought during the revolutionary era than any other philosopher. His writings were the colonists' major work of reference in their struggle with the mother country. The Declaration of Independence was so close to the Second Treatise of Government in form, phraseology, and content that Jefferson was accused of copying from it. Locke's influence can be seen in state declarations and constitutions. His ideas were present in the Philadelphia Convention. They played an important role thereafter, as well. Locke is the philosopher to whom the authors of the Federalist are most indebted for an exposition of constitutionalism and free government.

Summary and Analysis of Essay 38

Summary

Madison issues a scathing indictment of the proposed constitution's critics. He conjectures that ancient civilizations often entrusted the writing of their constitutions to a single man since they were afraid of the "discord and disunion among a number of counselors" more so than the "treachery or incapacity in a single individual."

Madison systematically lays out several different criticisms of the constitution made by the anti-federalists in order to illustrate the incoherence and inconsistency of the opposition's views. He asserts that the critics don't even agree on what is wrong with the proposed constitution and have failed to offer any better solution.

Madison furthermore argues that even if the proposed constitution has some defects, it is certainly better than the present form of government enshrined in the Articles of Confederation. He criticizes the Articles for "declaring certain powers in the federal government to be absolutely necessary" while "at the same time rendering them absolutely nugatory." That is, the Articles say the government ought to have a wide range responsibilities but has structured government in such a way as to deny the government the power to meet these responsibilities and function effectively. The core difference between the Articles and the proposed constitution are not the functions they are to perform but the powers they are granted to actually perform them.

Analysis

Madison's position can basically be summed up in a simple phrase: the means must match the ends. The problem with the Articles is that the government does not have the power to do its job. The Constitution fixes this by granting government that power, or "energy."

Madison employs the use of an analogy in this paper to illustrate his point. He compares America to a sick patient who seeks out the opinion of respected doctors. Eventually, these doctors come to agree unanimously on the cure, but several other people interject at the last minute that the cure will not work. These people agree the patient is sick, but oppose the cure while failing themselves to offer a viable alternative. The anti-federalists are these people in Madison's analogy.

Summary and Analysis of Essay 39

Summary

The purpose of this paper is to determine whether or not the framers established a republican form of government. No other form is suited to the particular genius of the American people; only a republican form of government can carry forward the principles fought for in the Revolution or demonstrate that self-government is both possible and practical.

Madison asks what are the distinctive characteristics of the republican form of government. Unfortunately, Madison continues, one cannot find the answer by reading certain books which purport to describe the constitutions of republican nations. Holland, Venice, and Poland are described by political writers as republics, but the power in all three governments is not derived from the people; it is held by kings, nobles, or a small group of people. Since the term "republic" is loosely used, we must look to the theoretical principles of republicanism as they have been defined.

A republican form of government is one which derives its powers either directly or indirectly from the people and is administered by persons who hold public office for a limited period of time or during good behavior. No government can be called republican that derives its power from a few people or from a favored and wealthy class. The Constitution conforms to these republican principles. The people directly elect the House of Representatives; in addition, the people indirectly select the senators and the president. Even the judges will reflect the choice of the people since the president appoints them, and the senate confirms their appointment. The president, senators, and representatives hold office for a specified and limited term; judges are appointed for life –but subject to good behavior. The constitutional prohibition against granting titles of nobility and the guarantee to the states that they shall enjoy a republican form of government is further proof that the new government is republican in nature.

These facts do not satisfy all people. Some people claim that the Convention destroyed the federal aspect of the government by taking away too much power from the states. According to these opponents, the framers established a national form of government,– one in which the citizens' are acted upon directly -- as citizens of the nation instead of citizens of the states. In reality, the proposed government contains both national and federal characteristics. It is true that the national government has authority over individuals as national citizens, but in many important respects the new plan of government is clearly federal in its form. The principle of federalism (division of power between the states and the national government) is reflected in the suggested method of ratification. The delegates to the ratifying conventions will vote as citizens of their states, not as citizens of the nation. The federal form is also reflected in the structure of the Senate in which the states are equally represented.

The fact that the states retain certain exclusive and important powers is further proof of the federal nature of the proposed government.

But, Madison says, we are not going to claim that there are no national features. Of course there are. Madison concludes that the government in its structure is both national and federal; in the operation of its powers, it is nation; in the extent of its power, it is federal.

Analysis

This essay, concerning the republican nature of the Constitution, is one essay that critics point to as having a "split personality" with previous essays that Hamilton had penned. Madison is more conciliatory towards the federal aspects of the government, while Hamilton only expounds on the nationalistic aspects of the new government. The split personality of the Federalist can be considered the root of the dualism that became so characteristic of American constitutional development. The disagreement over the nature of the Union may have contributed to nullification and succession or, for that matter, to the fight against these institutions. Likewise, Hamilton's and Madison's differing opinions on federalism were used when the Supreme Court interpreted the Constitution and largely account for that Court's oscillation between dual federalism and nationalism. Also, the authors different conceptions of the separation of powers seem to mark the beginning of a struggle between the legislative, executive, and judicial branches of government, evident throughout American history.

The originality of the Federalist papers, and the Constitution itself, means that these men were confronted with a genuinely democratic problem and succeeded in solving that problem, as Madison denotes here. This alone constitutes enormous progress in the theory and practice of government, as it existed up to their time. Former generations had been concerned largely with the question of how to restrict monarchial absolutism and had been confronted with the choice of monarchy or popular government. Hamilton, Madison, and Jay, on the other hand, conceived of popular government as the very premise for their arguments. They did not ask whether popular government should take the place of monarchy, as their predecessors had done. That question had been answered in 1776. Rather, they asked about the degree of democracy and majority rule.

Their answer was that of men who believed in the individualism of the English heritage and their intellectual environment. They bought forth their own concept of free government, under which the popular majority, while governing, was restricted by a constitution for the sake of the freedom of the individual and under which the democratic principle of popular participation in government, as a mere means, was subordinate to the liberal principle of the protection of the individual, as the end of government. Madison's description of the republican form of government is significant because it was such a noteworthy and novel concept in the time. The founders had solved the democratic problem in an ingenious manner, a problem that had plagued the European nations throughout the 19th and 20th centuries.

Summary and Analysis of Essay 40

Summary

Madison responds to the claim that the constitutional convention was authorized to frame and propose an entirely new form of government. Anti-Federalists charged that the convention had been formed to merely amend the Articles, not throw them out entirely in favor of the proposed constitution.

Madison argues that Congress had clearly authorized the convention to form a "a national and adequate government." Although it had only been explicitly instructed to accomplish this through "alterations and provisions in the articles of confederation," Madison argues that "alterations and provisions" alone would not be sufficient to achieve a "national and adequate government." Therefore, the convention rightly decided that it was more important to create the proper form of government than to limit itself to merely amending the Articles.

Madison argues further than the "great principles of the constitution proposed by the convention" are really just "the expansion of principles which are found in the articles of confederation." The problem with the Articles is that the principles were too "feeble and confined." All the Constitution does is empower the government to govern effectively on these principles.

Finally, Madison points to the fact that the Articles themselves were formed by a convention that was not explicitly authorized to do so. What matters ultimately, according to Madison, is whether the plans offered are good advice. The proposed constitution ought to be judged on its merits, not on the mere technicality of whether the convention was authorized to propose it.

Analysis

One of the many objections of the Anti-Federalists was that the Constitutional Convention had gone far beyond the authority granted to it by the states to amend the Articles. Madison is essentially dismissing this criticism as a technicality.

He acknowledges that the convention was not explicitly authorized to create an entirely new form of government, but asserts that the convention nevertheless acted in the best interests of the American people. Madison's argument, like most arguments contained in the Federalist Papers, is an appeal to pragmatism, common sense, and the greater good of the people, and a rejection of the mere technicalities and overzealous ideological quibbles on which the Anti-Federalists' arguments were based.

Summary and Analysis of Essay 41

Summary

Madison defends the powers granted to the national government in the proposed constitution. He structures his argument into two broad categories: the sum of power vested in government and the particular structure of the government. In this paper, he focuses on the first category and asks whether the "general" or national government has been granted too much power. He argues that it has not. In particular, Madison defends in detail the powers granted to Congress to declare war, grant letters of marque, provide armies and fleets, regulate the militia, raise taxes and borrow money.

Madison bases his argument on the principle that all forms of government are imperfect: "in every political institution, a power to advance the pubic happiness, involves a discretion which may be misapplied and abused." That is, governments must be given power in order to govern. However, by giving governments power, the people run the risk of that power being abused by government.

Madison illustrates this principle with reference to standing armies. He admits that they are dangerous to liberty, but nevertheless necessary to defend against foreign aggression. If Congress cannot raise armies in times of crisis, then Americans will fall prey to foreign invaders or internal disruptions. It is better to endure the risk of having a standing army than to be totally defenseless against hostile forces.

Madison furthermore contends that the power to raise armies and revenue cannot be limited because future threats and needs cannot be predicted. However, he reminds his readers that Congressional authority only extends to certain, enumerated powers.

Analysis

This paper introduces a series of papers that defend the extensive powers granted to the union by the Constitution. Madison takes a very systematic, highly structured approach to the presentation of his arguments. He begins the paper with an outline of the argument to follow and then expounds on each point in detail. This style differs somewhat from the Hamiltonian approach, which often lacks the careful, methodical approach of Madison.

Madison's essential goal in this paper is to address the concern that the federal government would have too much authority under the proposed constitution. What is striking about Madison's argument is that, rather than offer a glowing assessment of the virtues of a strong national government, he defends the central authority outlined in the Constitution as a necessary evil. He argues that granting any government any degree of power risks the government abusing that power. However, the alternative of a weak and ineffectual government is simply not an option. Without strong government, America cannot defend itself from foreign aggression, guarantee the rule of law or raise revenue to address national problems that transcend state boundaries.

Therefore, there is a central tension between liberty and strong government. On the one hand, liberty cannot long survive with a strong government to protect it from foreign aggression or domestic turmoil. On the other hand, strong government has the power not only to protect the people but to oppress them as well. Madison and the other founders argue, however, that the solution to this dilemma is to establish a strong government that is accountable to the people and subject to checks and balances that ensure it does not violate the rights of the people

Summary and Analysis of Essay 42

Summary

Madison defends two more classes of powers afforded to the general government: the regulation of intercourse with foreign nations and the regulation of intercourse among the states. Madison argues that the national government must be able to conduct diplomacy and act independently on the international stage just as all other nations do. It must be able to send and receive ambassadors, make binding treaties, and punish piracy.

Madison also discusses the provision in the Constitution allowing for the importation of slaves until 1808, after which Congress may decide to ban importation. It is very clear that Madison strongly opposes slavery as an inhumane and barbaric practice. However, he argues that while it would have been better to abolish the trade immediately, it is nevertheless better to place some sort of time limit on the trade than to leave it completely unfettered forever.

Madison goes into considerable detail in describing and defending the many specific powers granted to the general government to manage relations between the states. Perhaps the most important is the authority of the national government to regulate interstate commerce. Madison argues that if the national government is not authorized to perform this role, tensions and "serious interruptions of the public tranquility" will result from states imposing various kinds of taxes and restrictions on goods coming from other states.

Analysis

The powers of the national government described in these papers may strike modern readers as perfectly reasonable and perhaps even obvious. Of course a national government must be able to conduct diplomacy, regulate a single national currency, and serve as a final authority over issues of interstate commerce. However, this paper must be understood within the context of American colonial history.

Since their founding, the individual American colonies, although part of the British Empire, enjoyed a considerable amount of independence and self-government. In fact, the American Revolution was sparked in part by British attempts to limit the independence of the colonies. Consequently, after the war, many Americans were extremely suspicious of central governments with powers superior to the state governments. Madison is trying to make the case in this paper for why, if America is to be a strong, independent and cohesive nation, the states must be willing to accept the creation of a general government with considerable powers.

Madison also deals briefly with what may be considered one of the great moral failings of the constitution: the clause permitting the continuation of the slave trade until 1808. This stipulation was the result of a compromise between Southern states, the plantation economies of which depended on slave labor, and Northern states, the economies of which were based more on trade and industry and which were home to many anti-slavery activists.

Summary and Analysis of Essay 43

Summary

Madison explains and defends what he calls a "fourth class" of "miscellaneous powers." These include the power to grant patents and copyrights, the power to pass all laws governing the capital city and federal buildings, the power to determine the definition of and punishment for treason, and the power to admit new states. The national government is not allowed, however, to join two or more states or separate off part of a state to form a new state, without the consent of the states involved. Madison furthermore defends the power of Congress to make rules and regulations regarding territory and property belonging to the United States.

One of the most important powers Madison defends in this paper is the power of the national government to guarantee the republican form of government in each state and to protect each state against invasion and domestic violence. Madison argues that in a union, the political institutions of one state can impact the interests of another. Therefore, the union has the right to ensure that state governments retain the republican character that characterizes American political culture nationwide. Madison furthermore claims that it is possible that a combination of foreign intervention and other malicious forces may result in a majority of a particular state changing the form of its government. In such cases, it is necessary for a higher power, separated from the conflict, to protect the republican character of state government.

Madison furthermore defends as commonsense the power of Congress to pay off all debts acquired by the United States under the Articles and to provide for amendments to the Constitution to be ratified by the states. Finally, Madison defends the article declaring that the Constitution will come into effect once nine states ratify it. He asserts that it would be unfair and unwise to let the objections of a few states hold hostage the interests of the great majority.

Analysis

This paper continues Madison's methodical, highly detailed discussion of the specific powers granted to the national government under the Constitution. As in other papers, he uses evidence from European history and philosophy to support his position and counter the arguments of the anti-federalists that the proposed constitution granted too much power to the national government.

One of the central and most controversial themes of the Federalist Papers is the power of the national government over the individual states. In this paper, Madison advances the notion that the national government will serve as a guarantee of the republican character of the individual states. At the time, this was a somewhat radical notion. Not only would the national government have numerous powers over interstate commerce and relations with foreign powers, but it would also serve as a check on the internal political situation of the constituent states. Madison is therefore advocating the extension of federal authority into the very heart of state political systems. This was a dramatic increase of federal authority in comparison to the Articles of Confederation. Madison defends this power by arguing that the internal politics of a state can influence other states as well. That is, the loss of liberty in Massachusetts could affect the liberties of New Yorkers. Therefore, a higher authority was needed to guarantee certain basic political rights in the states themselves. This argument of Madison's is an interesting spin on the anti-federalists faith in states' rights. Madison is positing that states may not always be the essential guardians of liberty anti-federalists believe them to be.

Summary and Analysis of Essay 44

Summary

Madison discusses restrictions on the authority of the states. He defends the prohibition on states entering into treaties, authorizing ships to attack enemy ships, printing money, granting titles of nobility, imposing import and export duties without the consent of Congress, and passing bills of attainder, ex post facto laws, and laws "impairing the obligation of contracts." Madison describes many of these restrictions as so obviously proper as to be unnecessary of a long discussion. He defends the restriction on states printing money by asserting that if every state could regulate the value of money, "there might be as many different currencies as states; and thus, the intercourse among [states] would be impeded." He defends the prohibition on bills of attainder, ex post facto laws, and laws impairing the obligation of contracts as violations of personal rights and "contrary to the first principles of the social compact."

Madison also defends the "necessary and proper" clause and the supremacy clause of the Constitution as essential to give "efficacy" to all the other powers and provisions granted to the national government in the Constitution. He asserts that granting the union the right to make all laws "necessary and proper" to fulfilling its responsibilities is based on the simple principle that "wherever the end is required, the means are authorized." If a government has the authority to perform a particular function, it must necessarily have the power to do what is necessary and proper to perform that function. He defends the supremacy clause by asserting that it is a basic characteristic of government to have the authority to pass authoritative law.

Analysis

This paper concludes Madison's very methodical and careful defense of the specific powers granted to the union by the Constitution. Many of these powers had been discussed in previous papers, a fact which Madison acknowledges at several points. Such an approach reminds the readers that the Federalist Papers were not a single document, but a series of articles written in defense of the Constitution. They constituted part of a much larger national debate on the ratification of the Constitution. As in any debate, protagonists may restate their position at numerous points for emphasis or clarification.

Madison raises the stakes of the debate in the closing lines of this paper by asserting that the powers contained in the constitution are absolutely necessary for the preservation of the union: "the question, therefore, whether this amount of power shall be granted or not, resolves itself into another question, whether or not a government commensurate to the exigencies of the union, shall be established; or, in other words, whether the union itself shall be preserved."

Summary and Analysis of Essay 45

Summary

Madison argues that the powers granted to the national government by the Constitution do not threaten the powers left to the states. Madison asserts that state governments will lose some of their importance and sovereignty as a result of the Constitution. However, this is essential to the preservation of the union, which Madison asserts is essential to the public good.

Madison points to the history of confederations and feudal states to support his claim that the federal government will to "prove fatal to the state governments." Historically, "local sovereignties prevailed" in contests with central authorities. Madison then lists several reasons for why the state governments will continue to have significant power and relevance under the Constitution. He argues that, if anything, it is the federal government that is at greatest risk of being rendered feeble, as under the Articles. The Constitution corrects that problem by offering the federal government greater powers.

Madison closes by asserting that the powers granted to the federal government are not really "new powers" so much as an "invigoration" of the "original powers" granted to it by the Articles. The Constitution does not expand these powers. It just "substitutes a more effectual mode of administering them."

Analysis

Having established in previous papers the necessity of giving the national government all the powers described in the Constitution, Madison now seeks to reassure his audience that such a powerful general government will not threaten the remaining authority of the state governments and render them wholly subservient. This paper is further evidence of how suspicious the American people were of the proposed national government.

There is an inherent tension in Madison's argument. On the one hand he argues that there is an urgent need to invigorate the national government with sufficient power to govern effectively. The central failure of the Articles was the weakness of the central government. On the other hand, Madison labors to convince his audience that the state governments will still retain a significant degree of authority and will, in many respects, have a far greater impact on daily American life than the national government. This tension illustrates the central compromise between state and federal authority that serves as one of the key pillars of the American Constitution.

Summary and Analysis of Essay 46

Summary

Madison continues and concludes the argument begun in the previous paper. He asserts that the powers of the federal government under the proposed constitution will not threaten the powers reserved to the states.

Madison begins the paper by reminding his audience that the American people are the common superior of both the federal and state governments. These two different types of governments have different powers, intended for different purposes, but nevertheless subject to the ultimate control of the voters.

Madison then employs a series of arguments to convince his audience that the state governments have several natural advantages over the federal government in terms of securing the support of the people. State officials and representatives live in close daily contact with the electorate and deal with issues that directly impact their lives. Furthermore, just as representatives in state governments are typically biased towards their home counties and towns, so will representatives in Congress be biased towards their home states: "A local spirit will infallibly prevail much more in the members of the congress, than a national spirit will prevail in the legislatures of the particular states."

Furthermore, Madison argues that if the federal government were to encroach on the rights of the states, the latter would have a significant advantage in resisting such action. States could ultimately band together in resisting the federal government. Madison dismisses as highly unlikely the chances of the federal government being able to raise an army powerful enough to overcome all the state militias.

Analysis

Madison repeats arguments made in previous papers by Hamilton, asserting the many advantages state governments have over the federal government in terms of securing the support of the people and resisting encroachments.

Although in previous papers Madison labored to convince his readers that the system proposed by the constitution would lead to stable and energetic government, he describes at length in this paper a series of hypothetical conflicts between state and federal government. Madison clearly does not expect or hope the constitution to lead to the kinds of conflicts between state and federal authority described here. Rather, he seeks to establish that his opponents' "chimerical" predictions of federal authority crushing state governments are completely unfounded.

Summary and Analysis of Essay 47

Summary

James Madison begins this paper by telling his readers that he is going to examine a specific principle of republican government: "separation of powers." One of the principal objections to the constitution is that it violates this important principle. Its opponents claim that the three branches of government are not sufficiently separate and independent and that power is too unevenly distributed. It is feared that the new government will collapse, and that liberty will be threatened.

Madison agrees with those who place great importance on the separation of powers, especially on the point that an unequal division of power could result in the loss of liberty. If one branch has too much power, it does not matter how many men govern or how they obtain office. Too much power in one branch of government "is the very definition of tyranny." If these claims were true, Madison says that no other arguments would need oppose it. He, however, is convinced that this charge cannot be supported. How separate should each branch of government be?

Montesquieu, the French political writer, formulated this principle of government. He took the British constitution as his model, which he called "the mirror of political liberty." However, the most casual glance at that constitution reveals that the branches of the British government are far from totally separate or distinct. For example, the English king acts in a legislative capacity when he enters into treaties with foreign sovereigns: once treaties are signed they have the force of legislative acts. The English king not only appoints and removes judges; he frequently consults them. The judicial branch, then, acts in an advisory capacity to the executive branch. The legislative branch advises the king on constitutional matters and, in cases of impeachment, the Houses of Lords assumes judicial power. From these few facts, Madison infers that Montesquieu, when he wrote that "there can be no liberty where the legislative and executive powers are united in the same person . . . or, if the power of judging be not separated from the legislative and executive powers," did not mean that the powers should remain absolutely separate or that each branch should not have any control over the other branches.

Madison continues that if one looks at the state constitutions, there is no state in which the branches of government are absolutely separate and distinct. The state constitutions do not violate the separation of power doctrine set forth by Montesquieu, Madison concludes, and neither does the United States Constitution.

Analysis

In this essay, Madison clearly delineates his philosophy concerning separation of powers. Calling the accumulation of legislative, executive, and judicial power in the same hands - whether of one, of a few, or of many, and whether hereditary, self-appointed, or elective - the very definition of tyranny, Madison considers their separation essential to the preservation of liberty. He points out that when the legislative and executive powers are united there can be no liberty, because apprehensions may arise lest the same monarch or senate should enact tyrannical laws to execute them in a tyrannical manner. Furthermore, "were the power of judging joined with the legislative, the life and liberty of the subjects would be exposed to arbitrary control, for the judge would then be the legislator. Were it joined to the executive power, the judge might behave with all the violence of an oppressor."

This was not the only time that Madison had talked about the separation of powers. Before the first Congress, Madison said on June 17, 1789, that the principle of the separation of powers "is to be found in the political writings of the most celebrated civilians and is everywhere held as essential to the preservation of liberty . . . ; and if in any case they are blended, it is in order to admit a partial qualification, in order more effectually to guard against an entire consolidation."

The authors of the Federalist took a rather cautious attitude toward legislative supremacy. In their desire to secure free government, they were in favor of a system of government under which the legislature would not be more important than the other branches of government. This led them to follow the classic exponent of the separation of powers, Montesquieu. The Frenchman provided the additional machinery that was necessary to make a reality of the ideal of a government of laws and not of men, combined with the Lockeian concept of free government and the sacrosancity of property.

Summary and Analysis of Essay 48

Summary

Publius begins by telling the reader that we discussed some of the issues raised by the doctrine known as "separation of powers." This principle of republican government does not imply that the three branches need to be completely separate and independent. The very opposite is true. In order that this doctrine can operate effectively, each branch of government must have sufficient power to impose some restraints over the other two.

The Constitution grants to each branch certain exclusive powers. These powers should not be interfered with; however, power not carefully controlled tends to expand. Our first task, he writes, is to understand and distinguish the differences between legislative, executive, and judicial power. This is necessary to protect the legitimate powers of each branch.

It is not enough to simply set forth on paper what the proper boundaries are. There must be some latitude, some overlap, in the definition of powers assigned to each branch. Experience with state governments has shown that theoretical checks written into the state constitutions are inadequate, particularly in preventing the growth of legislative power. The most serious mistake made by the framers of republican forms of government is that they concerned themselves exclusively with the problem of too much executive power. They forgot that legislative tyranny is as evil as executive tyranny.

In hereditary monarchies the king is feared; in direct democracies the executive is also feared because the legislative branch is too large to effectively check the executive, and power is so highly diffused that conflicts are difficult to resolve. In direct democracies, the legislature cannot tyrannize because it cannot govern.

In the proposed government, however, it is the legislative branch that is most likely to abuse power. More power, both unrefined and unlimited, has been granted to it than to the other two branches. In addition, the legislative branch controls the money and has the greatest influence in the determination of salaries paid to government employees. Such a situation invites corruption. Presidential power, on the other hand, is simpler in nature, and the Constitution clearly defines and limits it. The same is true of judicial power. Any attempt by these two branches to infringe upon the Congress would be quickly detected and blocked.

Analysis

The idea of separation of powers was, of course, not new, nor novel to the founding fathers. Plato and Polybius were concerned with it in their discussion of a mixed state, and the concept of a tempered or mixed monarchy was a familiar one during the Middle Ages. In England, the struggle between the crown and the courts of common law, and between the crown and Parliament, had given concrete importance to the separation of powers. Harrington had considered it a prerequisite for free government, and Locke had given it a subsidiary role in his theory of parliamentary supremacy. However, the idea of mixed government had never had a definite meaning. It had connoted a balancing of social and economic interests, or a sharing of power by such corporations as communes or municipalities. Often, the concept was proposed as a remedy against extreme centralization and as a reminder that a political organization would only work if there existed some degree of comity and fair dealing between its various parts. It was Montesquieu who modified the ancient doctrines by making the separation of powers into a system of legal checks and balances between the parts of a constitution.

Montesquieu's idea, which was derived inductively from a study of the English constitution, gained a great deal of popularity in America. After having been hailed by the colonists in their attempts to curb the powers and prerogatives of the royal governor, the principle of the separation of powers was a guiding light for the constitution making that took place after independence had been declared. It was mentioned in the Virginia Declaration of Rights in 1776 and in the preamble of the constitution of Massachusetts of 1780, and it thus found official recognition in America years before it was put down in the famous article 16 of the French Declaration of the Rights of Man and Citizen. The members of the Philadelphia Convention reaffirmed the validity of the Montesquieuian concept, the more so since the preceding years had shown a lapse in its strict observance, which was due largely to the belief that a strong legislature, considered by many as the great liberator from monarchical despotism, could not very well be destructive of the Frenchman's ideal of liberty.

The Federalist accepts the framers' version of the separation of powers. Aware of the probability of legislative usurpations, the authors of that work desire a separation that would be likely to eliminate legislative supremacy. No matter how much Hamilton and Madison might disagree on certain aspects of the separation of powers, they see eye to eye with respect to that major point. Montesquieu's influence on the Papers, however, goes still further. Not only is his idea of a separation of the executive, legislative, and judicial branches accepted, but also his concept of checks and balances. Montesqieu seems to have had a special fascination of the authors, especially for Madison. This popularity may have been due partly to Montesquieu's inductive method, which was likely to have a certain appeal to statesmen who were, in a way, suspicious of mere philosophical speculations. However, what probably accounts most for Hamilton's, Madison's, and Jay's sympathy for the Frenchman was the fact that he chose the English constitution as an example of the merits of a separation of powers. Montesquieu thus became the great foreign herald of the rights of Englishmen. These were the rights that our authors believed in, that they hoped would exist in the free government under the Constitution.

Summary and Analysis of Essay 49

Summary

After Jefferson finished writing "Notes on the State of Virginia," he added a rough draft of a constitution he hoped would be adopted at a state constitutional convention held in 1783. This draft constitution, like everything Jefferson wrote, is original and comprehensive. It is especially pertinent because Jefferson draws our attention to the weaknesses, as well as to the strengths, of a republican form of government. One of his proposals, intended to prevent one branch of government from becoming too powerful, is unique, but the writer has some criticism of it. He recommends that a constitutional convention should be held whenever two branches of government, by a two-thirds vote, desire to change the Constitution or correct any violation in it.

Since the people are the source of power in a republican form of government, it would seem logical to consult them whenever one branch becomes too powerful or whenever there is a constitutional crisis. But there are problems in relying on the people to keep each branch within its constitutional limits. In the first place, the people cannot prevent the possibility of two branches combining their strength and power against the third branch. In the second place, frequent appeals to the people suggest a serious defect in government. Such appeals threaten the stability necessary to good government because society is always in a state of turmoil. Although Madison concedes that this country has been successful in revising its form of government, too much experimentation can be dangerous. Because the revolution is behind the country, divergent views and strong disagreements are coming to the surface.

Madison continues that it is evident that the legislative branch is most likely to seize power from the other two branches. The appeals of the people would, therefore, come from either the executive or the judicial branch. But those branches combined are smaller than the legislative branch, and the people are not as familiar with them. The judicial branch, in particular, is far removed from the people because justices are appointed, rather than elected, and serve for life; the people will always view the president with certain skepticism; every administration will be subject to a degree of unpopularity and distortion. By contrast, members of the legislative branch move freely among the people and are connected to them by ties of blood and friendship. The representatives are elected by the people and are the most responsive to their wishes. Furthermore, they are regarded as the chief defenders of the peoples' rights and liberties. For these reasons it is doubtful that the executive and judicial branches could enlist the sympathies of the people. Not only could the legislators plead their cause most successfully, they would dominate the very conventions called to air the grievances against them.

Analysis

In this essay, more than any other besides perhaps 51, Madison lays out his philosophy on free government. Madison does not state in the Federalist how the state of nature is abandoned and government created. We may assume, however, that his opinion does not differ here from what has been called the core of his philosophy, namely the compact theory of the foundation of the state. This theory was generally accepted at the time the essays were written, whereas the organic theory was hardly known. Madison adhered to it even when it was being abandoned by most European theorists, and called it a "fundamental principle of free government." Furthermore, the acceptance of the compact theory in the Federalist can be concluded from the fact that Madison, who recognizes a parallel between the formation of the state by individuals and the formation of a confederacy by state, calls the Confederation "a compact among the States."

Madison's view on the relation between people and government has important consequences. His conception of government as a means follows not only the primacy of the individual's protection before popular participation in government, but also his Federalist, advocating the Union, can be a treatise on the Union only in a relative sense and must, in an absolute sense, be a treatise for individual rights. His conception of society as an intrastate phenomenon must influence his view on the nature of confederations and the Union. Finally, from the necessity of the independence of the government from the people follows the possibility that government abuses it power. In that case the people, possessing "the transcendent and precious right . .. . to abolish or alter their governments as to them shall most likely to effect their safety and happiness (62)" may resort to a revolution. Furthermore, from the subjection of government under a constitution follows the existence of two sorts of man-made law; that by which the government is bound (society-made, fundamental, constitutional law), and that by which the government binds the people (government-made, ordinary, statue law).

In summary, Madison believed that the individuals, motivated by self-interest, leave the state of nature in order to live under justice in a free government that, primarily, protects their lives, liberty, and property and,– to the degree compatible with the security of these rights, permit people to participate in government under a constitution. The main threat to free government arises form its own creation of factions, the control of which is of vital importance. The latter observation has important implications for Madison's inquiry into the compatibility of concrete governments with the ideal free government. In his search for the government that is most likely to realize that ideal, he need only look for a government under which factions are controlled.

Summary and Analysis of Essay 50

Summary

Madison rejects the proposal to allow for periodical, or regular, appeals to the people as a means of "preventing and correcting infractions of the constitution." At the time, some had proposed adding to the constitution certain provisions allowing for the government to be subjected to some sort of public examination on a regular basis to ensure that it is not violating the constitution. However, Madison doubts that this will be successful. He suggests that if the intervals between the examinations are too short, it will be difficult for the people to be impartial since "the measures to be reviewed and rectified…will be connected with all the circumstances which tend to vitiate and pervert the result of occasional revisions." If the intervals are too long, however, the distant possibility of public censure will not be an adequate check on the behavior of government officials.

Madison supports his position with the example of a council of censors that met in Pennsylvania in 1783 and 1784 for the purpose of revising the state constitution "in order to correct recent breaches of it." This failed in part because the members of the council were not impartial, were motivated by passion rather than reason, and were themselves been members of government within the period to be reviewed.

Analysis

Madison appears to be very careful in rejecting these calls for periodic public examinations of government conduct. He must be careful because such a proposal is deeply republican in character. The anti-federalists had been accusing the federalists of trying to undermine republican principles with the creation of an overly powerful national government. Therefore, if Madison appears to be staking out an anti-republican position, he risks losing public support.

Madison recognizes in this and previous papers the value of holding government accountable to the people. However, he asserts that the kind of public censuring proposed here will be ultimately ineffective. Although an advocate of the separation of powers and checks and balances, this is one check on government power that Madison does not support.

Summary and Analysis of Essay 51

Summary

James Madison begins his famous federalist paper by explaining that the purpose of this essay is to help the readers understand how the structure of the proposed government makes liberty possible. Each branch should be, in Madison's opinion, mostly independent. To assure such independence, no one branch should have too much power in selecting members of the other two branches. If this principle were strictly followed, it would mean that the citizens should select the president, the legislators, and the judges. But the framers recognized certain practical difficulties in making every office elective. In particular, the judicial branch would suffer because the average person is not aware of the qualifications judges should possess. Judges should have great ability, but also be free of political pressures. Since federal judges are appointed for life, their thinking will not be influenced by the president who appoints them, nor the senators whose consent the president will seek.

The members of each branch should not be too dependent on the members of the other two branches in the determination of their salaries. The best security against a gradual concentration of power in any one branch is to provide constitutional safeguards that would make such concentration difficult. The constitutional rights of all must check one man's personal interests and ambitions. We may not like to admit that men abuse power, but the very need for government itself proves they do: "if men were angels, no government would be necessary." Unfortunately, all men are imperfect, the rulers and the ruled. Consequently, the great problem in framing a government is that the government must be able to control the people, but equally important, must be forced to control itself. The dependence of the government on the will of the people is undoubtedly the best control, but experience teaches that other controls are necessary.

Dividing power helps to check its growth in any one direction, but power cannot be divided absolutely equally. In the republican form of government, the legislative branch tends to be the most powerful. That is why the framers divided the Congress into two branches, the House of Representatives and the Senate, and provided for a different method of election in each branch. Further safeguards against legislative tyranny may be necessary.

In a representative democracy it is not only important to guard against the oppression of rulers, it is equally important to guard against the injustice which may be inflicted by certain citizens or groups. Majorities often threaten the rights of minorities. There are only two methods of avoiding evil. The first is to construct a powerful government, a "community will." Such a "will' is larger than, and independent of, the simple majority. This "solution" is dangerous because such a government might throw its power behind a group in society working against the public good. In our country, the authority to govern comes from the entire society. In addition, under the

Constitution society is divided into many groups of people who hold different views and have different interests. This makes it very difficult for one group to dominate or threaten the minority groups.

Justice is the purpose of government and civil society. If government allows or encourages strong groups to combine together against the weak, liberty will be lost and anarchy will result. And the condition of anarchy tempts even strong individuals and groups to submit to any form of government, no matter how bad, which they hope will protect them as well as the weak.

Madison concludes that self-government flourishes in a large country containing many different groups. Some countries are too large for self-government, but the proposed plan modifies the federal principle enough to make self-government both possible and practical in the Untied States.

Analysis

In this essay, Madison's thoughts on factionalism are delineated clearly. As we observed earlier, he assumed that conflicts of interests are inherent in human nature, and he recognized that, as a consequence, people fall into various groups. He wanted to avoid a situation in which any one group controlled the decisions of a society. Free elections and the majority principle protected the country from dictatorship, that is, the tyranny of a minority. However, he was equally concerned about the greater risk of tyranny of the majority. A central institutional issue for him was how to minimize this risk.

Madison's solution characteristically relied not only on formal institutions, which could be designed, but also on the particular sociological structure of American society, which he took as a fortunate starting point for the framers of the new constitution. The institutional component in his solution was checks and balances, so that there were multiple entry points into the government and multiple ways to offset the power that any one branch of the government might otherwise acquire over another. In this system, "the constant aim is to divide and arrange the several offices in such a manner as that each may be a check on each other."

These institutional arrangements were reinforced by the sociological fact that the Republic contained a multiplicity of interests that could, and did, offset one another: "While all authority in it will be derived from and dependent on the society, the society itself will be broken into so many parts, interests and classes of citizens that the rights of individuals, or of the minority, will be in little danger from interested combinations of the majority." It is good that there are many group interests; that they be numerous is less important than that they be impermanent and shifting alliances whose components vary with the specific policy issue.

Madison commenced the statement of his theory in Federalist 51 with an acknowledgement that the "have nots" in any society are extremely likely to attack the "haves." Like Hamilton, the Virginian believed class struggle to be inseparable from politics. "It is of great importance in a republic not only to guard against the oppression of its rulers," Madison writes, "but to guard one part of the society against the injustice of the other. Different interests necessarily exist in different classes of citizens. If a majority be united by a common interest the rights of the minority will be insecure."

Madison, it is clear, had emancipated himself from the sterile dualistic view of society that was so common in the eighteenth century and that so obsessed Hamilton. Madison was one of the pioneers of "pluralism" in political thought. Where Hamilton saw the corporate spirit of the several states as poisonous to the union, Madison was aware that the preservation of the state governments could serve the cause of both liberty and union. Finally, the vastness of the United States, a fact that Hamilton considered the prime excuse for autocracy, was recognized by Madison as the surest preservative of liberty. To assert after reading this passage that Alexander Hamilton wrote Federalist 51 is to imply, first, that he was a magician in mimicking Madison's very words and tone of vote, and second that he was the most disingenuous hypocrite that ever wrote on politics. No unprejudiced or informed historian would accept this latter charge against Hamilton.

It is interesting to note that the Federalist papers are unique, as shown in this paper, because of the extreme amount of thought that was put into the design of the Constitution, as shown in Madison's original thought process that were penned in 51. Many, if not most, changes in institutional design, occur as the reactions of shortsighted people to what they perceive as more-or-less short-range needs. This is one reason the Constitutional Convention was a remarkable event. The Founding Fathers set out deliberately to design the form of government that would be most likely to bring about the long-range goals that they envisaged for the Republic. What is most unusual about Madison, in contrast to the other delegates, is the degree to which he thought about the principles behind the institutions he preferred. Not only did he practice the art of what nowadays is deemed institutional design, but he developed, as well, the outlines of a theory of institutional design that culminated in this essay.

Summary and Analysis of Essay 52

Summary

Madison explains the Constitution's provisions for electing members of the House of Representatives. He discusses the importance of a constitutionally-guaranteed right to vote and details the qualifications candidates must have to be elected.

Madison devotes the majority of the paper to a discussion of the "safety" of biennial elections. By safety, Madison means the protection of liberty from a tyrannical government. Madison uses examples from British, Irish, and American history to defend the prudence of electing representatives every two years. He asserts that such a system will guarantee that the representatives remain beholden to the American people, first and foremost.

Analysis

The frequency of congressional elections was an important part of the debate over the proposed Constitution. Some Americans felt that elections ought to be held on a yearly basis in order to ensure that representatives remain under the control of their constituents. Others argued that elections should be held less frequently in order to improve the stability and efficiency of government. Biennial elections represent a compromise between these two positions.

Madison's approach to this discussion is somewhat imprecise. He does not offer any specific evidence guaranteeing that biennial elections are the best protection against a tyrannical legislature. Rather, he deduces from historical examples that they must be safe. For example, he suggests that if British liberty could be secured with triennial elections, surely American elections would be secured by even more frequent elections.

Summary and Analysis of Essay 53

Summary

Madison continues his defense of biennial elections for members of the House. He rejects the notion that liberty is confined to a "single point of time" and that elections must take place annually in order to minimize the risk of tyranny. He points to the fact that elections occur with varying frequency in the different states without any discernible difference in the degree of liberty enjoyed by each state.

Madison suggests further that since the Congress cannot change the fundamental form of government (i.e. amend the Constitution) on its own, there is less risk in having elections on a biennial instead of annual basis. Madison furthermore suggests that it takes time for congressmen to understand the complex issues facing them at the federal. One year would be insufficient for acquiring sufficient knowledge to make informed decisions.

Finally, Madison points to certain practical issues, such as the inconvenience of traveling long distances to Congress to serve only a one year term. He also warns that one year would not afford enough time to remove from office congressmen who took office through fraudulent or illegitimate means in order to accomplish some corrupt agenda.

Analysis

Madison seeks to reassure his readers that their liberty will be secure under the proposed Constitution. He appeals to his audience's pragmatism and asks them to think critically about the widely held assumption that the safest form of republican government is one in which the representatives are elected annually. He reminds them that the American Congress will be different from previous republican legislatures in that it will be limited in its powers by a supreme law, the Constitution. Unlike the British parliament, Congress cannot change the fundamental law of the land by a mere legislative act. Thus, there is little cause to fear that, in the span of two years, elected representatives of the people will succeed in imposing tyranny.

This paper illustrates an interesting tension between the ideals of republican liberty and the practical necessities of modern government. In the republican ideal, citizens would essential govern themselves in small polities with all men playing an active role in political life. Insisting on annual elections was one way of ensuring that power would always remain in the hands of voters and not become to concentrated in distant politicians. Madison does not challenge these republican virtues, but argues instead that, in order for government to actually be effective, some practical compromises are necessary.

Summary and Analysis of Essay 54

Summary

Madison defends the constitution's system for apportioning representatives among the States according to population. He also discusses the decision to count slaves as three-fifths of a person. He gives several reasons for the compromise: that the laws regard slaves as both property and persons; that southern states would consider it unfair to include slaves in calculating tax burdens but not for the number of representatives apportioned to the states; and that it would take into account the different levels of wealth of the states. Madison admits that this reasoning is somewhat of a stretch; however, it asserts that it was a "compromising expedient" necessary to pass a constitution acceptable to all states.

Finally, Madison suggests that by basing both taxes and number of representatives on population, the Constitution ensures states do not have an incentive to manipulate the numbers. If states claim too small a population, they will benefit in terms of taxes, but suffer in terms of the number of representatives they are allotted.

Analysis

This paper deals with what is often considered one of the great moral failures of the Constitution: the three-fifths compromise. Madison's discomfort with this compromise is palpable. In explaining the reasoning behind the compromise, he assumes the voice of his "Southern Brethren" rather than accept full responsibility for the arguments himself: "Such is the reasoning which an advocate from the southern interests might employ on this subject."

The question of how to count slaves for the purposes of taxes and apportionment of representatives was deeply controversial and split the northern and southern states. Madison's treatment of this topic illustrates his personal discomfort with the existence of slavery in the United States. At various points in the paper, Madison refers to slavery as a degrading to human dignity and a great misfortune.

Summary and Analysis of Essay 55

Summary

Madison defends the size of the House of Representatives. Critics had alleged that there were too few members of the House to guard against the cabals, i.e. small groups of legislators violating the rights of the people. Madison argues that the House is big enough to guard against such cabals and small enough to avoid the inefficiencies and confusion of a multitude. Madison points to the fact that the size of state legislatures vary greatly to suggest that the exact size of the House need not be restricted to a precise number.

Madison also introduces the notion that republican government ultimately depends on the virtue of the people. Without virtue, "nothing less than the chains of despotism can restrain them from destroying and devouring one another."

Analysis

This paper is the first of four dealing with the major criticisms leveled against the House of Representatives. He seeks to present his opponent's arguments as unreasonable and exaggerated. According to Madison, the legislature's quality does not necessarily increase in direct proportion to its size: "Had every Athenian citizen been a Socrates, every Athenian assembly would still have been a mob."

Madison's discussion of virtue, though relatively brief, is very important. One of the advantages enjoyed by the anti-federalists was their ability to imagine all the varied ways in which corrupt or power-hungry politicians could use their constitutionally granted powers to threaten the rights of the people. While the federalists' arguments were confined to what was actually contained in the Constitution, the anti-federalists could come up with all sorts of worst case scenarios. Madison seeks to undercut this strategy by pointing out that no republican government can provide 100% security against usurpations. At some point, the people must have a certain degree of virtue to ensure the safety of the republic.

Summary and Analysis of Essay 56

Summary

This paper answers a second criticism levied against the House: that it is too small to possess adequate knowledge of the interests of the people. Madison responds that the representatives only need to have adequate local knowledge as it pertains to commerce, taxation, and the militia. Other, more minute details, "do not lie within the compass of legislation." Madison argues that in all three of these areas, Congress will have enough members to make informed decisions on these issues.

Madison argues that congressmen need to be more concerned with adequately understanding issues in other states and making proper legislation as it relates to them. That will be their major task. However, as the country continues to develop, Madison suggests the interests in the states will become relatively similar even as the complexities within the States themselves increase.

Analysis

This paper echoes the argument Madison makes in the tenth paper, that a relatively small number of representatives will be capable of comprehending national issues since these issues will be general in nature. In taking this approach, Madison reminds his audience that the powers of the national government are not unlimited. They only pertain to certain, general issues affecting the country as a whole. Questions of concern to particular states will in most circumstances be dealt with the state governments, which will presumably have the necessary local knowledge.

This paper's argument illustrates the important concept of federalism: the sharing of power between national and state governments. Representatives in Congress would not need to have intimate knowledge of local conditions in particular states since their primary responsibility would be to regulate issues that affect all states and the interaction between states. It was left to the state governments to deal with issues relevant only to particular localities.

Madison also advances the hypothesis that, over time, the interests of states will become increasingly the same. History has shown this to have been a very prescient observation. Although present-day American states do at times deal with issues particular to their population, Americans increasingly identify as "Americans" rather than as residents of a particular state. 21st century Americans are much more conscious of their national character than 18th century Americans were. At the time of the Constitution's adoption, many Americans felt more loyalty to their state than to the union, and economic, cultural, and social differences between the states were much more pronounced than they are today.

Summary and Analysis of Essay 57

Summary

Madison answers the charge that the House of Representatives will consist of people who "will have least sympathy with the mass of the people; and be most likely to aim at an ambitious sacrifice of the many, to the aggrandizement of the few." Madison points out that the electors of the representatives will not be confined to certain segments of the population, but will consist of "the great body of the people of the United States."

Madison then outlines several reasons for why the representatives will remain faithful to the interests of the American people. He argues that a sense of duty, gratitude, interest, and ambition will ensure that the representatives serve the people well. In particular, he notes that the representatives owe their distinguished position to the people and, especially due to the frequency of elections, will be motivated to retain their support. If they want to stay in power, the representatives must behave properly in the eyes of the people.

Analysis

Madison seeks to address popular fears of oligarchy, or rule by a few. Americans, forever jealous of their liberty and suspicious of government, needed to be assured that this new, powerful national government would not use its authority to violate the interests of the people.

Madison employs two distinct strategies in seeking to allay these suspicious. First, he takes a very logical approach, backed up by examples from both the English system of government and the state governments, to show that the government outlined in the proposed constitution contains sufficient safeguards to protect against a tyrannical legislature.

However, he also appeals to the American "spirit," which he describes as "vigilant and manly...a spirit which nourishes freedom." This is the ultimate safeguard against encroachments on liberty by the government. Animated by this spirit, the American people would never tolerate attempts by the legislature to advance the interests of a few over those of the many.

Summary and Analysis of Essay 58

Summary

Madison responds to concerns that the number of members of the House will not be increased as population growth demands. Many opponents of the Constitution in larger states were concerned that the smaller states would seek to limit the increase in the number of members allotted to each state based on population. In particular, they feared that the Senate, which gives a disproportionate amount of power to smaller states, would become an instrument for limiting increases in the number of representatives in the House so as to restrict the power of larger States.

Madison presents several arguments for why this will not be in the case. Perhaps most importantly, the House, where larger states have the greatest influence, holds the power of the purse. Only the House can propose bills for funding the government. Thus, if the Senate or President tried to restrict the expansion of the House's membership, it could use its power of the purse to persuade these other branches of government to relent.

Madison also returns to his previous argument, that the safety of the republic does not necessarily increase in direct proportion to the number of elected representatives. He argues that in a large assembly, it is easy for a few powerful orators or demagogues to persuade the multitude of representatives to support a particular policy that may not be beneficial to the public good.

Analysis

This paper again illustrates the significant tension and mutual suspicion that existed between the large and small states during the debate over the Constitution. In this paper, Madison is primarily addressing the fears of the large states, of which New York was one of the most important. He tries to reassure them that the small states will not be able to unduly limit their representation.

The concern over tensions between large and small states may strike the 21st century American as somewhat odd. The issues that animate the public consciousness today rarely center around tensions between large and small states. However, in the 18th century, many Americans felt a greater attachment to their state than to the nation. As a result, they were deeply suspicious of any Constitutional provisions that might grant an undue source of power or influence over them to another state.

Additionally, think of modern problems with the electoral system, which gives a huge amount of influence in the election of the president to large states. States with many electoral votes, like Texas, Florida, and California, are able to single-handedly swing a presidential election. As a result, campaigning is focused in these states, and smaller states are ignored. The tension between large and small states continues to be very present today in these matters.

Summary and Analysis for Essay 52

Summary:

In this paper, Madison explains the Constitution's provisions for electing members of the House of Representatives. He discusses the importance of a constitutionally-guaranteed right to vote and details the qualifications candidates must have to be elected.

Madison devotes the majority of the paper to a discussion of the "safety" of biennial elections. By safety, Madison means the protection of liberty from a tyrannical government. Madison uses examples from British, Irish, and American history to defend the prudence of electing representatives very two years. He asserts that such a system will guarantee that the representatives remain beholden to the American people first and foremost.

Analysis:

The frequency of congressional elections was an important part of the debate over the proposed Constitution. Some Americans felt that elections ought to be held on a yearly basis in order to ensure that representatives remain under the control of their constituents. Others argued that elections should be held less frequently in order to improve the stability and efficiency of government. Biennial elections represent a compromise between these two positions.

Madison's approach to this discussion is somewhat imprecise. He does not offer any specific evidence guaranteeing that biennial elections are the best protection against a tyrannical legislature. Rather he deduces from historical examples that they must be safe. For example, he suggests that if British liberty could be secured with triennial elections, surely American elections would be secured by even more frequent elections.

Summary and Analysis for Essay 53

Summary:

In this paper, Madison continues his defense of biennial elections for members of the House. He rejects the notion that liberty is confined to a "single point of time" and that elections must take place annually in order to minimize the risk of tyranny. He points to the fact that elections occur with varying frequency in the different states without any discernable difference in the degree of liberty enjoyed by each state.

Madison suggests further that since the congress cannot change the fundamental form of government (i.e. amend the constitution) on its own, there is less risk in having elections on a biennial instead of annual basis. Madison furthermore suggests that it takes time for congresspersons to understand the complex issues facing them at the federal. One year would be insufficient for acquiring sufficient knowledge to make informed decisions.

Finally, Madison points to certain practical issues such as the inconvenience of traveling long distances to congress to serve only a one year term. He also warns that one year would not afford enough time to remove from office congresspersons who took office through fraudulent or illegitimate means in order to accomplish some corrupt agenda.

Analysis:

Madison seeks to reassure his readers that their liberty will be secure under the proposed Constitution. He appeals to his audience's pragmatism and asks them to think critically about the widely held assumption that the safest form of republican government is one in which the representatives are elected annually. He reminds them that the American Congress will be different from previous republican legislatures in that it will be limited in its powers by a supreme law, the Constitution. Unlike the British parliament, Congress cannot change the fundamental law of the land by a mere legislative act. Thus, there is little cause to fear that, in the span of two years, elected representatives of the people will succeed in imposing tyranny.

Summary and Analysis for Essay 54

Summary:

In this paper, Madison defends the constitution's system for apportioning representatives among the States according to population. He also discusses the decision to count slaves as three-fifths of a person. He gives several reasons for the compromise: first, that the laws regard slaves as both property and persons; that southern states would consider it unfair to include slaves in calculating tax burdens but not for the number of representatives apportioned to the states; and that it would take into account the different levels of wealth of the states. Madison admits that this reasoning is somewhat of a stretch; however, it asserts that it was a "compromising expedient" necessary to pass a constitution acceptable to all states.

Finally, Madison suggests that by basing both taxes and number of representatives on population, the Constitution ensures states do not have an incentive to manipulate the numbers. If states claim too small a population, they will benefit in terms of taxes, but suffer in terms of the number of representatives they are allotted.

Analysis:

This paper deals with what is often considered one of the great moral failures of the Constitution: the three-fifths compromise. Madison's discomfort with this compromise is palpable. In explaining the reasoning behind the compromise, he assumes the voice of his "Southern Brethren" rather than accept full responsibility for the arguments himself: "Such is the reasoning which an advocate fro the southern interests might employ on this subject."

The question of how to count slaves for the purposes of taxes and apportionment of representatives was deeply controversial and split the northern and southern states. Madison's treatment of this topic illustrates his personal discomfort with the existence of slavery in the US. At various points in the paper, Madison refers to slavery as a degrading to human dignity and a great misfortune.

Summary and Analysis of Essay 59

Summary

Hamilton defends the provision in the Constitution for national control over the scheduling and regulation of elections to the House. He argues that if state governments were given control over national elections, then the national government would find itself at the mercy of states. Hamilton does recognize that state governments do have the right to control the elections of senators and that this creates the opportunity for states to delay or prevent the election of senators. However, he argues that this was a necessary compromise so as to maintain the federal principle of shared power between the states and the national government.

Hamilton sees no reason for extending this risk to include the House, especially since the House is elected every two years. If House elections were delayed, it would be truly detrimental. In contrast, senators are elected every six years and only one third of all Senate seats are up for election every two years. Thus, even if certain states tried to prevent an election from taking place, it would difficult for them to completely shut down the Senate.

Analysis

Perhaps the most striking part of this paper is Hamilton's admission that allowing state legislatures to control elections of senators "is an evil." He describes this evil as one that could not be avoided since to do so would exclude the states "from a place in the organization of the national government." This discussion illustrates the importance of federalism in the American system of government. The states and the union share power. They are not entirely distinct from one another, but, in certain respects, interdependent.

Summary and Analysis of Essay 60

Summary

Hamilton responds to concerns that the power of the national government to determine the time, places, and manner of elections of representatives to the House might result in the elevation of the wealthy over the mass of the citizens. The fear seems to have been that the national government may conspire to hold elections in only parts of the states populated by the wealthy. This would presumably prevent lower income citizens from voting.

Hamilton rejects this fear on several grounds, including the fact that such places do not exist—that is, the rich are scattered throughout the states. Hamilton also argues that the American people would never tolerate such behavior by the national government. He furthermore asserts that the separation of powers between the House, the Senate and the president would make it much more difficult for the national government to conspire against the states. Each branch of the national government is elected by different populations—the House by the people, the senate by the state legislatures (though this was later changed by the 17th amendment) and the president by electors chosen by the people. Given the fact that each branch has such different sources of power, it would be highly unlikely for them to all represent a particular class of people or a particular set of interests.

Analysis

This paper illustrates the primacy of the separation of powers to the American form of government. Hamilton contends that, unlike other national governments, the American government is unlikely to fall into the control of a single class of citizens since there are numerous branches of government that must share power.

This paper furthermore reasserts Hamilton's fundamental faith in the republican form of government. No usurpation of power by the national government would be possible because the people, motivated by a love for liberty and conscious of their rights, would not allow it. Finally, this paper captures the complicated operation of federalism, or separation of power between the states and the national government.

Hamilton concludes the paper by taking his opponents' arguments to their logical extreme. This tactic is an attempt to demonstrate the exaggerated and unreasonable fears of his opponents. He notes that even if the national government somehow succeeded in rigging elections, it would not even be necessary since they would presumably have gained enough power to usurp the rights of the people directly without recourse to elections.

Summary and Analysis of Essay 61

Summary

In this paper, Hamilton responds to the claim that the Constitution should have required elections to be held in the counties where the electors reside. This would prevent Congress from forcing States to hold elections in a location inconvenient to the voters, or a certain segment of voters.

Hamilton responds that in many state constitutions, including New York's, there is no such provision for the location of elections and that no harm resulted from this omission.

Furthermore, Hamilton asserts that there will be a significant advantage in allowing Congress to set a uniform time for elections to be held. He argues that placing the entire house and one third of the senate before the people for reelection at the same time will help ensure that the same detrimental "spirit" or "faction" will not continue for long in Congress. He speculates that if each state could hold elections at different times, then members of Congress would be added and removed gradually and thus make new members, few in number, susceptible to pressure from the majority of Congress to support a particular faction detrimental to the public good.

Analysis

Hamilton suggests that the issue discussed in this paper ought not to be considered significant enough to hold up the ratification of the entire Constitution. He admits that it would not really have been detrimental if the Constitution had included a provision specifying where elections were to be held in the States. However, he suggests that it was not really necessary either. He therefore dismisses the critics who use this issue as a justification for opposing the constitution as partisans of a "predetermined opposition." His opponents are not candidly attempting to "research after truth" but merely to obstruct the passing of the Constitution with petty and insignificant objections.

Hamilton also expands on the important theme of "faction" discussed in earlier papers. One of the core concerns of the founders was that a particular faction, or interest group, would succeed in obtaining undue influence over the government. It was particularly feared that a particular "spirit of faction," such as temporary but intense support for a narrow political position, could take over the government and lead to the adoption of laws detrimental to the rights and interests of the people. However, by requiring most of the Congress to stand for election every two years, the Constitution gives the American people ample opportunity to remove from office politicians who support these factions.

Summary and Analysis of Essay 62

Summary:

Madison begins this paper explaining that it will examine four points concerning the Senate; the qualification of the senators, the method by which they are selected; equal representation in the Senate; and the number of senators and the six-year term.

Two differences exist between the qualifications of senators and representatives: senators must be older and must be citizens of the United States longer. Senators serve longer and need a broader knowledge of government affairs, particularly in the area of foreign relations; consequently, the framers thought they should be older. Appointment by the state legislatures, rather than election by the people, is desirable for two reasons: first, this type of appointment assures that the Senate will consist of a select group of men, and the appointment by the states will provide a link between the states and the national government.

The Constitution provides for two senators from each state. This equality of representation is clearly a compromise between the different interests of the large and small states. In a federal system (where power is share between the states and the national government), it would be unfair not to recognize two opposing principles – proportional versus equal representation. The principle of proportional representation is recognized in the House; the principle of equal representation is recognized in the Senate. Equal representation in the Senate protects the sovereignty of all the states, thus ensuring that the new government will not abolish the state governments. It also means that a bill, which must be passed by both houses before it becomes a law, will reflect the whishes of the people (represented by the House) and the states (represented by the Senate).

The method of appointing the senators solves another important problem. Frequently, men who hold public office forget their obligation to the people, and therefore, betray the public trust. By dividing the legislative branch into two parts and requiring agreement between them, the liberties of the people will be more secure, and the passage of bad laws will be more difficult. The history of governments all over the world demonstrates that where the legislative body is not divided their partisan leaders often sway the legislators. The senate, which consists of fewer men who will hold their office for six years, reduce this threat. Representatives, elected by the people, serve for only two years; in many cases their private occupations may be more important to them than their public office, and they cannot be expect to devote sufficient time to government or to a study of the laws. Most blunders of our governments to date have been caused by incompetence and a lack of political wisdom.

The Senate will not only provide stability in government, it will reduce the tendency of the House to pass too many laws. Unnecessary legislation produces chaos and favors the wealthy. The people cannot be expected to keep up with too many new laws and regulations; farmers and merchants will be reluctant to start new business ventures if they feel that new regulations will hurt their investments.

The object of good government is the happiness of the people, but good intentions are not enough. Our state and national governments have paid too little attention of statecraft and the art of government. Fortunately, the structure of the government under the Constitution will help to correct this defect. A society cannot progress unless the government is stable and respectable.

Analysis:

There can be little doubt that the designers of the Constitution saw good public policy and stability in the laws as paramount concerns. In Federalist 62, for example, Madison defended the Senate in the proposed bicameral Congress on the grounds, in part, that the Senate could block passage of undesirable polices which a unicameral legislature might approve: "Another advantage accruing from this ingredient in the constitution of the Senate is the additional impediment it must prove against improper acts of legislation. No law or resolution can now be passed without the concurrence, first, of a majority of the people, and then of a majority of the States." Similarly, "a Senate, as a second branch of the legislative assembly distinct from and dividing the power with a first, must be in all cases a salutary check on the government. It doubles the security to the people by requiring the concurrence of two distinct bodies in schemes of usurpation or perfidy, where the ambition or corruption of one would otherwise be sufficient."

One reason that House members could not always be trusted stemmed from their short terms of office. To Madison, this meant that these legislators would be unable to develop the necessary wisdom about public policy. As he remarked about the virtues of a Senate whose members have longer terms, "Another defect to be supplied by a senate lies in a want of due acquaintance with the objects and principles of legislation. It is not possible that an assembly of men called for the most part from pursuits of a private nature continued in appointment for a short time and led by no permanent motive to devote the internals of public occupation to a study of the laws, the affairs, and the comprehensive interests of their country, should, if left wholly to themselves, escape a variety of important errors in the exercise of their legislative trust." It was thought that a Senate with a slow turnover and whose members had long terms of office would be able to avoid the unwise polices that a unicameral legislature might be expected to produce.

A bicameral legislature could also be expected to help prevent instability in the laws. There was no doubt in Madison's mind that instability in the laws had great costs: "To trace the mischievous effects of a mutable government would fill a volume." These effects were both external and internal. Externally, instability causes the nation to forfeit "the respect and confidence of other nations." Internally, the consequences of instability were even worse – "it poisons the blessings of liberty itself." Commerce could also expect to suffer from an unstable government.

In 1785, the Marquis de Condorcet published his Essai, in which he explicitly noted and discussed the particular problem of majority rule instability. While The Federalists do not specifically discuss the problems of majority rule instability, one scholar notes that Madison had read Condorcet's essay and is known to have written a review of it, a review which is now, unfortunately, lost. Although not explicitly, therefore, Madison and the Federalist papers do internally deal with instability, especially within Federalist 62 and the instability of the legislature branch.

Summary and Analysis of Essay 63

Summary:

Madison continues this essay where he left off, claming that the fifth desire of the utility of a Senate is the "want of a due sense of national character." To any foreign country, it is necessary to have a strong, perceptive senate to ensure respect and confidence. Other nation's opinions are important for two reasons: first, that a plan will appeal to other countries as a wise policy and second, the opinion of the world, in difficult situations, can be followed. Yet, however important national character is, the Senate cannot be a numerous and changeable body. It must be small enough so that public opinion can guide each of the members, as well as pride in their actions, because of the great amount of public trust in the body.

A sixth defect is the want of responsibility in the government to the people, because of the frequency of elections and other cases. The Senate, however, solves this defect because it is in power long enough to be responsible for the decisions that it makes.

The Senate is not a well-conceived idea, however, merely because it represents the people. It is also a good idea because at times the people need to be protected from their own ideas and prejudices. Although people are spread over an extensive region, they can still be "subject to the infection of violent passions"

In addition, "history informs us of no long lived republic which had not a senate." They, however, had senates elected for life. America, however, will not follow these examples because they are repugnant to the foundations upon which the country is built. The plan of the senate, however, blends the stability with the ideal of liberty. A senate, however, is still extremely important and necessary because they then represent the people but are immune from the people's whims. The people must be represented and in a senate that sits for life, this does not occur.

Some people, however, argue that six years is to long and leads to tyrannical situations. Madison answers, however, that in order for the Senate to corrupt, it must corrupt itself, the state legislatures, the House of Representatives, and the people at large. It, therefore, is not possible in only six years. If the people do not believe Madison, they should look at the examples of the State Constitution, particularly Maryland, which has a strong senate that has not corrupted the rest of the state. The best example, however, is Britain's House of Lords, a hereditary assembly, which has not infected the rest of the country. With the balance of the House of Representative to guard and represent the people, the Senate is a necessary and important function of government that will support the "people themselves."

Analysis:

In order to effectively understand James Madison's argument in this federalist paper, it is necessary to understand the constitution's opponent's critique of the senate. Anti-Federalists argued that the Senate was too powerful and aristocratic. Federal farmer argued that, "The formation of the senate, and the smallness of the house, being, therefore, the result of our situation, and the actual state of things, the evils which may attend the exercise of many powers in this national government may be considered as without remedy." Likewise, Centinel lamented that the Senate is "the great efficient body in this plan of government" and that it "is constitution on the most unequal principles." Cincinatus summed up the critique quite well: "We have seen powers, in every branch of government, in violation of all principle and all safety condensed in this aristocratic senate; we have seen the representative or democratic branch, weakened exactly in proportion to the strengthening of the aristocratic."

This Federalist paper defends the Senate as providing the wisdom and the stability – "aristocracy virtues" – needed to check the fickle lack of wisdom that Madison predicated would characterize the people's branch of the new government, the lower house. Nor were there other critics lacking who, recognizing that the Constitution ultimately rested on popular consent, who, seeing that despite the ingenious apparatus designed to temper the popular will by introducing into the compound modified monarchial/aristocratic ingredients, could argue that the new Constitution was too democratic to operate effectively as a national government in a country as large and with a population as diverse and the Americans'. One such was William Grayson, who doubted the need of any national government but who felt, if one was to be established, it ought to provide a president and a Senate elected for life terms, these to be balanced by a House of Representative elected triennially.

It is significant, therefore, to notice that present day critics of the Constitution argue about the exact nature of the Constitution, just as they did in 1787 and 1788. It is easy to see and disagree on whether the constitution is monarchical, aristocratic, or democratic in its essence. John Adams probably best described the constitution, however, in 1806, writing to Benjamin Rush. Adams, disapproving of Jefferson's style as president, bemoaned the fact that Jefferson and his followers had made the national government "to all intents and purposes, in virtue, spirit, and effect a democracy." -- Alas! "I once thought," sad Adams "our Constitution was quasi or mixed government."

An additional important note about this paper is Madison's use of the word "responsibility." According to the Oxford English Dictionary on Historical Principles the word itself is an American invention, and its first appearance in the language is credited by the OED long discussion of senatorial "responsibility" in Federalist Number 63. The word appears four times in two paragraphs, as well as in Hamilton's Number 70 and 77, as the differences between senatorial responsibility, presidential responsibility, and judicial responsibility are discussed in these issues.

Summary and Analysis of Essay 64

Summary

In this paper, Jay defends the provision in the Constitution granting power to the president to make treaties with the consent of two thirds of the Senate. He argues that it was important to give this power to the president and Senate, which he argues will consist of the "most enlightened and respectable citizens," given the minimum age requirements for their office, as well as other factors. Jay contends that it is better to trust these responsibilities to the Senate than the House since the members of the former are elected less frequently and to longer terms. This allows them to acquire the extensive knowledge necessary for handling such grave matters as treaties with other nations. Another advantage of this system, according to Jay, is that it allows the president to conduct negotiations in secrecy and then, at an appropriate point, get the advice of the senate.

Jay responds to objections that the treaties ought to be amendable by legislative acts by arguing that treaties are fundamentally different from regular laws. They must be binding on the American people and not subject to change by a mere act of Congress. Otherwise, other nations may not be willing to enter into treaties with the US.

Analysis

This paper illustrates the founders' attempts to reconcile the republican values of the American people with the realities of international diplomacy. There is a need for stability in foreign policy making. Otherwise, foreign nations will be unable to trust the US to abide by the terms of its treaties. Furthermore, international relations are deeply complex and serious issues that must be handled with "secrecy" and "dispatch." American foreign policy, according to Jay, would be hamstrung if the President did not have the ability to conduct secret negotiations with foreign governments and take advantage of rare opportunities in international affairs. This very practical need for granting significant powers to the executive is nevertheless offset by the requirement that all treaties be ratified by the senate. We thus see in this aspect of the American system of government a balance struck between expediency and republican suspicions of excessive power in the executive branch.

At this point in history, many Americans were deeply suspicious of foreign powers and wary about becoming entangled in foreign alliances and international crises. George Washington warned that America should avoid becoming excessively intertwined with the endless machinations and power politics of European powers. Instead, he thought Americans should strive to maintain their neutrality and independence. Anti-federalists were concerned that granting too much authority to the president and the Senate in international affairs would open the door to corruption and shady deals with foreign powers. However, Jay tries to convince

Americans that the Constitution adopts a balanced approach to this issue.

Summary and Analysis of Essay 65

Summary

Hamilton defends the use of the Senate as a court of impeachment for public officials impeached by the House of Representatives. He argues that there are certainly disadvantages to having a political institution serve as judges given the significant potential for partiality. However, the Senate is the best option available. The Supreme Court would be inadequate due to its small size and the fact that an official, once removed from office, might then find himself judged in criminal court by the same judges who removed him from office.

Hamilton also dismisses the idea of having a separate institution or collection of officials to serve as a court of impeachment. He warns that such a body would be too expensive.

Analysis

This paper is striking in its admission of imperfection. Hamilton acknowledges that having a political body serve as a court creates the possibility of politically motivated trials of public officials. However, he believes the Senate is the best available option for fulfilling this necessary role. This argument serves as a reminder that the defenders of the Constitution did not necessarily consider it a perfect document, but merely the best available and far superior to the Articles. Hamilton expresses frustration with critics who attempt to hold up the ratification of the Constitution on the basis of small imperfections that are inevitably parts of any system of government.

In the interesting to note that the provisions in the Constitution for removing officials from office have been relatively rarely used. In fact, less than two dozen federal officials have been impeached in American history, and even fewer have been removed from office. Only two presidents have been impeached, Andrew Johnson and Bill Clinton, but both were acquitted by by the Senate.

Summary and Analysis of Essay 66

Summary

Hamilton responds to four further objections raised against the powers granted to the Senate as a court for the trial of impeachment. The first objection is that the provision "confounds legislative and judiciary authorities in the same body." Hamilton argues that this is necessary and proper since the congress must be able to hold the executive accountable. He further notes that the role of accusing and judging is split between the two houses of Congress and that similar systems have been used in the states without deleterious effect.

The second objection is that the Senate will have so much power as to become aristocratic in a nature. Hamilton argues that the house will have sufficient powers to counter the influence of the senate. The third objection is that the senators will not be able to impartially judge presidential appointees who they once voted to confirm. Hamilton argues that the Senate will not be so biased as to be blind to the "evidences of guilt so extraordinary" as to have induced the representatives in the House to have impeached the official.

The fourth objection is that senators will not be able to impartially judge themselves for the role they play in the ratification of foreign treaties. The critics imagine a situation in which senators act corruptly in ratifying a certain treaty. These critics claim that in such a situation the senators would end up being their own judges. Hamilton dismisses this on the basis that it would likely be only a few corrupt leaders in the senate who manipulated the treaty and that these men could be impeached and tried. He furthermore points out the rather obvious impossibility of fashioning a system in which a legislative body could impeach or convict itself by majority vote.

Analysis

That the Senate would eventually become an American aristocracy was a central argument of the anti-federalists. This argument was particularly power in the context of recent American history. The country had just fought a war to rid itself of the imperial yoke placed on them by Great Britain, a country known to have a powerful and extensive aristocracy. Americans at this time were deeply suspicious of political bodies that could become the center of power for a select segment of society.

In this final paper devoted to defending the constitutional provisions for the Senate, Hamilton takes these accusations on directly and seeks to show that the Constitution has numerous protections and limits on the powers of the Senate. He seeks to show that a diversity of competing interests would keep the Senate from successfully conspiring to threaten American liberty. Much of Hamilton's argument is based on the role played by the House of Representatives in limiting the power of the Senate.

The House was seen as a more democratic body directly accountable to the people since, in the original Constitution, only the members of the House were directly elected by the people. Senators, on the contrary, were chosen by state legislatures.

Summary and Analysis of Essay 67

Summary

Hamilton forcefully accuses the anti-federalists of misrepresenting the provisions in the Constitution relating to the presidency. He accuses the critics of misleading the American people and playing on their fears of monarchy in order to turn them against the Constitution. As evidence of this deception, Hamilton conducts a close reading the sections of the Constitution dealing with the powers of the presidency and focuses on dispelling the false claim that the president would have the power to appoint vacancies in the Senate.

Analysis

This is the first of eleven papers in which Hamilton defends the office of the presidency as described in the proposed constitution. The presidency was perhaps the most controversial aspect of the proposed form of government. Anti-federalists accused the federalists of seeking to recreate a monarchy through the creation of a president with extensive executive powers. These claims were particularly worrisome to the American people since they had just fought a war to rid themselves of a monarchy they considered tyrannical.

Hamilton does not offer his opponents the benefit of the doubt. He questions not only the soundness of their arguments but also the goodness of their intentions. His strategy in this paper is to show, in exhaustive detail, that his opponents are purposely misinterpreting and distorting the meaning of the Constitution in order to convince the American people that it will lead to a despotic, tyrannical form of government.

Summary and Analysis of Essay 68

Summary

Hamilton defends the process for selecting the president. He argues that the system of an electoral college ensures that "the sense of the people" will play a key role in selecting the president, while, at the same time, affording "as little opportunity as possible to tumult and disorder." It was believed that electing the president directly, without the intermediate step of the electors, might lead to instability. Hamilton argues that electors will be protected from bias since they do not hold any other political office and are separated from electors from other states. Hamilton believed that this system would best ensure that the president was a man of great virtue and ability.

This paper also discusses the provisions for the House of Representatives to elect the president in cases in which no candidate receives a majority of the votes. It furthermore defends the decision to elect the vice-president in much the same way that the president is elected.

Analysis

This paper presents one of the more peculiar aspects of the American Constitution: the electoral college. Although in modern American politics, the electoral college is seen by some as an archaic and unnecessary relic of an earlier time, it illustrates the founders' fundamental concerns about stability.

One of the inherent weaknesses in a government based on the will of the people is the potential for mob rule. This was often the downfall of direct democracies, where all the people decided on public matters directly rather than through representatives. In designing the electoral college, the founders sought to insulate the selection of president from the convulsions of the multitudes. The college was essentially an extra layer of security helping to guarantee that the president would be a truly capable individual.

Summary and Analysis of Essay 69

Summary

Hamilton seeks to counter claims that the president would be an "elective monarch" as the anti-federalists claimed. Hamilton points to the fact that the president is elected, whereas the king of England inherits his position. The president furthermore has only a qualified negative on legislative acts—i.e. his veto can be overturned—whereas the king has an absolute negative. Both the president and the king serve as commander in chief, but the king also has the power to raise and maintain armies—a power reserved for the legislature in America. The president can only make treaties with the approval of the Senate. The king can make binding treaties as he sees fit. Similarly, the president can only appoint officers with the approval of the Senate, whereas the king can grant whatever titles he likes. The powers of the president in terms of commerce and currency are severely limited, whereas the king is "in several respects the arbiter of commerce."

Hamilton furthermore suggests that, in many respects, the president would have less powers over his constituents than the governor of New York has over his.

Analysis

Hamilton structures his argument around a three-way comparison of the office of the presidency under the proposed constitution, the king of England, and the governor of New York. Hamilton's chief concern is to counter claims that the president would have powers commensurate to the English monarch against whom Americans fought a war. He does this in a very specific and methodical way, taking a variety of issues and comparing the powers of the president and the king.

In order to make the argument more relevant to the people of New York, who Hamilton is addressing, he introduces a comparison between the president and the governor of New York as well. Surely, the people of New York would not claim that the president under the proposed constitution is an elected monarch if his powers are roughly commensurate to their own governor.

Summary and Analysis of Essay 70

Summary

Many people think that a vigorous and strong president is incompatible with a republican form of government. Hamilton, however, does not agree. An energetic and forceful president is essential to good government. National defense, sound administration of the law, and the protection of property rights all depend upon the vitality of the Presidency. In addition, an energetic president best protects liberty when faction, anarchy, and the excessive ambitions of others threaten it. Anyone familiar with Roman history knows that it was often the Roman dictator who prevented the fall of the council. Men agree that the president should be strong. What, then constitutes strength and energy? What characteristics do we look for? Can sufficient strength in the Presidency be combined with the principles of republican government?

An energetic executive branch must be characterized by unity, sufficient powers, and a certain degree of secrecy. For these reasons, one chief executive is better than two or more. Two people, granted equal power and authority, are bound to differ. Personal ambition can never be totally subdued, and a dual presidency would be marked by dissension, weakened authority, and the growth of conflicting factions. It is unnecessary and unwise to establish an executive branch that would make this form of divisiveness possible and likely. Conflict and argument are dangerous in the executive branch where decisions must be prompt; in the Congress, on the other hand, differences of opinion force discussion and deliberation. This is quite proper in the legislative branch and helps to prevent coercion by majority. The function of the legislature is to pass laws; once a law is passed, effective opposition comes to an end. But the executive branch is charged with the execution of the laws; a law once passed should be executed promptly. Furthermore, in case of war, when so much depends upon a strong presidency, divisiveness could destroy the national security.

The same arguments against having two presidents can be made in opposition to an executive council. In either a plural or council form of executive, faults and defects are more easily concealed, and no person can be held responsible. The American president, unlike the English king, must not be immune from censure, accountability, or punishment. The English king is not held responsible for his administration, and his person is sacred. Sometimes a king forms a council to act as a buffer between him and his subjects. But such a council in no way diminished the king's power; he is not even bound by the resolutions the council passes. The council functions as a public relations body while, at the same time, it protects the king in his absolute power.

In conclusion, Hamilton claims that there is the matter of expense. Those who recommend a council form of executive admit that the council should be large. That being so, the salaries of the council members would constitute too great an expense for the nation to tolerate. Second, before the Constitution was written, intelligent men agreed that New York's single executive was one of the most admirable features of state government.

Analysis

This essay concerning the powers of the executive department is one of the most referenced federalist papers concerning the presidency. Hamilton writes, "energy in the executive" is one of the most important parts of the executive department of the country, as defined in the Constitution. This "energy" is one of the most written about components and excuses for expansion of presidential power, especially in the 20th century. If the Federalist Papers can be said to have "themes," one of those themes would be the importance of energy in making the Constitution come alive. In this essay, Hamilton demonstrates the necessity energy is to the president and his duties. The office and power of the president was consciously designed to provide the energy, secrecy, and dispatch traditionally associated with the monarchial form.

Another important aspect of this essay is the evidence of the proportion and participation principles and their relation to each other in the state. Since Hamilton considers the individual's protection the end of the government, an explanation of the protection principle can be derived from his specification of that end. In other Federalist Papers, Hamilton claims that with government being instituted for the distribution of justice, the end of government is "the public happiness" or the "public good." More specifically, the people's happiness means the protection of their "general liberty," their "rights." From his distinction between liberty and property and life and property follows Hamilton's classification of those rights into the categories commonly used in his time, namely, the rights of life, liberty, and property.

Of these rights, those of property are most important. Their greater weight, as compared with the rights of liberty, follows Hamilton's enumeration, in order of importance, of the advantages of an energetic executive. He mentions, first, the protection of the community against foreign attacks; second, the steady administration of the laws; third, the protection of property against irregular and high-handed combinations that sometimes interrupt the ordinary courts of justice; and fourth, the security of liberty. Hamilton thus puts the protection of property before the security of liberty and connects it more closely with that all-embracing end of government, justice. The prevalence of property before liberty is confirmed when Hamilton states that among vested rights, those concerning life and property are most important. When, finally, he refers hardly ever to the right of life and very often to that of property, the conclusion can be drawn that either he considers the right of life to be already accepted, or he attributes a greater weight to the right of property, which he once referred to as "the great and fundamental distinction of society."

Summary and Analysis of Essay 71

Summary

Hamilton defends the provision of the constitution for a presidential term of four-years. Some alleged that this was too long a term and would increase the risk of the president amassing too much power. However, Hamilton defends the four-year term from the perspective of energy. He argues that a term of four years will give the president the ability to counteract temporary passions or influences of faction that may from time to time convulse the American people and their representatives in Congress. It is the duty of the executive, according to Hamilton, to protect the interests of the people and the greater good of the nation, even when the people may, as a result of being deceived or manipulated, demand the adoption of flawed policy.

Hamilton furthermore argues that a term of four years will enable the president to pursue policies he feels best. If the term were too short, the president might not be willing to make bold, perhaps controversial decisions since to do so would risk incurring the ire of the people and perhaps cost him reelection.

Analysis

This paper continues Hamilton's defense of energy in the office of the presidency. Hamilton believed that having an energetic executive—that is, a president with true power and influence—was essential to building a strong union. He is trying to strike a balance between the republican values, which emphasize the role of the people's will in making policy, and the need for stable, effective and wise government. Hamilton asserts that the republican principle does not require that government act on "every sudden breeze of passion" that may influence the views of the people. Although the people usually "intend the public good," they do not always "reason right about the means of promoting it." Therefore, it is essential that the executive have sufficient independence and power to wisely determine the public good and counterbalance the influence of the less stable and more excitable legislature.

Predictably, Hamilton's position roused the ire of the anti-federalists, who often valued liberty and independence over stability and efficiency. Throughout modern history, many political scientists and historians have commented on the inherent tension between the supremacy of popular opinion and the preservation of political stability. Alexis D'Tocqueville, for example, warned about the risk of a "dictatorship of the majority" in democratic systems. Since democratic systems are fundamentally based on the will of the people, there is always a risk that the majority faction will adopt policies that seem wise but are actually disastrous. Hamilton felt it was important to have a strong executive at the top to counterbalance such excesses.

Summary and Analysis of Essay 72

Summary

In this paper, Hamilton defends the provision allowing for the reelection of the president to an unlimited number of terms. Hamilton argues that restricting the president to a single term or require him to spend time out of office before serving another term would have several ill effects. First, it would lead to too many disruptive changes in the many different aspects of the executive branch of government as each new president brought in his own set of advisers and assistants. The limitation would also diminish "inducements to good behavior" since the president would not have to worry about getting reelected. Prohibiting reelection might also tempt the president to usurp power rather than give it up voluntarily.

Hamilton argues further that the country needs experienced executives. By limiting the president to one term, the country would not enjoy the benefits of having a highly experienced president in office. It would be especially detrimental to deny the American people the leadership of a talented and experienced executive in a time of national crisis. Hamilton imagines a situation in which the president must leave office at the outbreak of war. A final downside would be the instability caused by such frequent changes of the chief magistrate.

Hamilton believes that the American people ought to have the option to continue in the office of the presidency any qualified man they want. Although there might be some advantage in term limits, such as greater independence of a president who is not concerned about being judged on his record and the greater protection afforded to the people against tyrants, Hamilton suggests these advantages are questionable.

Analysis

Hamilton's arguments in this paper follow naturally from the previous paper in which he defended the four-year length of presidential terms. Hamilton is attempting to overcome concerns that the president will become an American king. Although Hamilton clearly does not favor monarchy, he does advocate for an energetic and powerful executive. After all, the lack of a strong executive was one of the chief failings of the Articles of Confederation.

Although the original constitution did not place limits on the number of terms a president may serve, the 22nd amendment, enacted in 1951, limited presidents to a maximum of two terms in office. This amendment was passed after President Franklin Roosevelt was elected to four terms as president.

Summary and Analysis of Essay 73

Summary

Hamilton discusses the provisions in the Constitution guaranteeing a salary for the president that cannot be adjusted by Congress during his term and defends the president's right to veto congressional legislation. Hamilton contends that if the president's salary could be raised or lowered by Congress during his term, the legislative branch would gain an undue degree of power over the executive.

Hamilton defends the presidential veto by pointing to the necessity of holding legislative authority in check. He warns that Congress may at various points be convulsed by the influence of faction and, as a result, seek to pass laws detrimental to the public interest. In such situations, it is necessary for the president to be able to obstruct such legislation. Hamilton claims that in a republican society the executive will always hesitate to overrule the decisions of the legislative branch. He also points out that the veto is only a qualified negative; that is, the congress can override the veto with a two-thirds vote in both houses.

Analysis

This paper illustrates the principle of checks and balances on which much of the Constitution is based. The founders believed it was necessary to distribute power among multiple branches of government and ensure that none of these branches became too powerful. This paper focuses in particular on limiting the power of the legislature. Hamilton claims that, in republican societies, the legislative branch of government is always the most powerful since it directly represents the voice of the people. In order to prevent this branch from completely monopolizing the government, the other branches must have means of constitutional "self-defense."

Thus, in many respects, the Constitution was designed to produce conflict among the branches. The founders felt that it was important to design a system in which one locus of power would compete with another so as to prevent the rise of tyranny or the rash implementation of policies detrimental to the public good.

Summary and Analysis of Essay 74

Summary

In this short paper, Hamilton defends the power of the president to serve as commander-in-chief of the armed forces and to grant reprieves and pardons. Hamilton argues that the demands of war require a single supreme leader. A distribution of military authority among multiple, supreme executives could lead to disaster.

Although Hamilton considers the advantages that may be had from requiring pardons to receive legislative support, Hamilton ultimately decides that questions of mercy are best decided by a single executive. He implies that if pardons were to be decided by a group of individuals, they may feel less pressure to either grant mercy on humanitarian terms or to uphold justice when the circumstances of the case demand it. Furthermore, the judgment of Congress might be colored by partisanship. He furthermore imagines situations in which it will be essential to the national interest for the president to be able to grant pardons swiftly. For example, in order to "restore the tranquility of the commonwealth," it may be necessary for the president to grant a pardon to rebel leaders. If this process were delayed by the need to obtain congressional approval, important opportunities might be lost.

Analysis

The anti-federalists were deeply concerned that the presidential pardon would be misused just as royal pardons were frequently abused in Europe. The first high-profile pardon was issued by President Washington to the leaders of the Whiskey Rebellion in return for their renouncement of violent opposition to US law. Therefore this early use of the pardon affirmed Hamilton's claim that this particular power of the president would at times be essential to restoring peace and public order during times of domestic upheaval.

Since the early days of the republic, the presidential pardon has at times been highly controversial with some claiming that pardons tend to be issued for political reasons rather than concerns about mercy or justice. Today, applications for pardons are made to the office of the pardon attorney, an official of the US Department of Justice.

Summary and Analysis of Essay 75

Summary

Hamilton defends the treaty-making procedures outlined in the Constitution. He responds to the criticism that the Constitution wrongly mixes the legislative and executive branches of government by affording both a role in making and approving treaties. Hamilton argues that act of treaty-making does not fit neatly into the typical purview of either the executive or legislative branch. Therefore, affording a role to both is appropriate.

Other critics claimed that the power to make treaties should be limited to the president. Hamilton responds that, unlike European monarchs, the president is only in office for a limited period of time. He may therefore be tempted to sign a treaty detrimental to the nation but beneficial to his private interests since he will eventually return to being a private citizen (unlike monarchs). It is therefore necessary that his power be held in check by the legislature.

Others asserted that the Congress should have even greater authority over treaty making. However, Hamilton responds that this would introduce unnecessary delays and inefficiencies to the process and weaken the American negotiating position.

Analysis

This paper returns to an argument that had been previously addressed by other papers: the Constitutional provisions for treaty making. It illustrates the underlying tension built into the Constitution between the energy of government and the separation of powers. On the one hand, the founders wanted to ensure that the executive would be strong enough to negotiate effectively with foreign powers. If the president were too weak, other heads of state might not take him seriously. At the same time, however, the founders wanted to ensure that the president did not become too powerful—hence the role afforded to the Senate in ratifying treaties with foreign powers.

This paper also illuminates one of the most important assumptions underlying the entire American Constitutional system: men are not angels. The founders assumed that politicians would always be tempted to use their power for private gain, even at the expense of the public good. The founders feared that if the President had sole authority to make treaties, as European monarchs do, then he would be tempted to use that power for his own benefit. For example, imagine if present-day Presidents could sign trade agreements with foreign powers that resulted in substantial profits for a corporation in which the President had a personal financial interest. Without the supervisory role played by the Senate, there would be nothing to stop Presidents from using their treaty-making powers as little more than opportunities for self-aggrandizement.

Summary and Analysis of Essay 76

Summary

Hamilton defends the power of the president to appoint public officials with the advice and consent of the Senate. Hamilton argues that there are only three options for arranging the "power of appointment." The power can be entrusted to a single man, a select assembly or a single man with the concurrence of the assembly. Hamilton rejects the first two options. An assembly is likely to be subject to the influence of faction and partisanship, making difficult any impartial selection of officers on the basis of merit. On the other hand, leaving the decision to a single man might result in favoritism and corruption clouding the selection of officers. According to Hamilton, granting the nominating power to the president and the ratifying power to the senate is the best strategy for avoiding these defects.

Another objection to this arrangement centered on fears that the president would be able to pressure the senate to support a corrupt or unfit candidate. In response, Hamilton asserts that there will always be at least some virtue in the senators to ensure this does not happen.

Analysis

Once again, this paper illustrates the importance of the guiding principles of separation of powers and checks and balances. Hamilton sees potential for defects in both the presidency and the Senate. Therefore, neither can be entrusted with all the power of appointment. This further underscores the important role compromise and pragmatism played in the design of the Constitution. The founders never claimed that the political system they created would be perfect or risk-free. Rather, they were animated by the belief that the only reliable way to limit abuses of power was to ensure that the various branches of government had both the incentive and the ability to keep an eye on one another.

It is interesting to note that Hamilton's prediction of partisan concerns delaying or complicating the appointment of public officials has come true in recent American history. It is not uncommon for the appointment of officials to key positions in the national bureaucracy to be held up by political opponents of the president. Hamilton had hoped that giving the Senate power to approve presidential appointees would serve as a check on corruption. Unfortunately, senators in both political parties have often used their powers over the ratification process as a way to score cheap political points. Appointments are often held up on the basis of political squabbles rather than concerns about the appointee's character or fitness for office.

Summary and Analysis of Essay 77

Summary

In this final paper on presidential power, Hamilton answers some remaining objections leveled against the executive branch by the anti-federalists. He first speaks of the importance of stability in the administration of the government as a justification for requiring Senate approval to appoint or displace public officials.

He then devotes most of the paper to rejecting the notion that the Senate would have undue influence over the executive in the appointment of officials. He argues that the various honors and emoluments enjoyed by the office of the presidency would more likely grant the president influence over the Senate than the other way around. The role of the Senate is to restrain the president in his powers of appointment when necessary. This does not constitute undue influence. Furthermore, by arranging the power of appointment in such a way as to require both the executive and the legislature to play a role, the constitution essentially guarantees that appointments will become matters of notoriety and thus subject to public scrutiny.

Hamilton compares the appointment process called for in the Constitution to the process observed in the State of New York in order to demonstrate the dangers that would attend to entrusting the process to the complete control of a small council, whose decisions would not be subject to a legislative ratification process. Hamilton asserts that this results in favoritism and corruption dominating the process.

Hamilton concludes this section by claiming that the constitutional provisions for the presidency have successfully incorporated "all the requisites of energy" without violating republican principles of liberty. According to Hamilton, the president will have enough powers to be effective but can still be held accountable (e.g. through impeachment) by the people's representatives in the legislature.

Analysis

This paper brings to a close a series of papers defending the powers granted to the executive branch and the limits placed on that power. The key principle here is a balance between the need for a powerful and energetic executive, something lacking in the Articles of Confederation, with the imperative of ensuring that the executive does not have enough power to threaten American liberty.

By citing the example of New York State's process for appointing public officials, Hamilton tries to make this debate more accessible to his New York audience. He makes the somewhat bold assertion that the form of government proposed by the Constitution is superior to New York's. This example would have been very familiar to Hamilton's audience.

This paper serves as a reminder that, when analyzing the Federalist Papers, it is important to keep in mind that they were originally published as a series of newspaper editorials intended to convince New Yorkers to ratify the proposed constitution. If one approaches the Papers as a single volume or book addressed to a national audience or later generations of Americans, he or she is likely to be left very confused. Although the Federalist Papers were loosely organized around distinct topics and issues, the individual papers cite a wide range of issues and concerns that are often not directly connected to one another. This reflects the fact that the papers were part of an ongoing public discourse that constantly changed and evolved. The authors were responding to specific criticisms levied against the Constitution by the anti-federalists, who were themselves a large and loosely organized group with disparate concerns and interests. Thus, when studying the Federalist Papers, one of the core challenges for the reader is to distill the broad, unifying themes that tie together the specific arguments advanced by the individual papers.

Summary and Analysis of Essay 78

Summary

Hamilton begins by telling the readers that this paper will discuss the importance of an independent judicial branch and the meaning of judicial review. The Constitution proposes the federal judges hold their office for life, subject to good behavior. Hamilton laughs at anyone who questions that life tenure is the most valuable advance in the theory of representative government. Permanency in office frees judges from political pressures and prevents invasions on judicial power by the president and Congress.

The judicial branch of government is by far the weakest branch. The judicial branch posses only the power to judge, not to act, and even its judgments or decisions depend upon the executive branch to carry them out. Political rights are least threatened by the judicial branch. On occasion, the courts may unfairly treat an individual, but they, in general, can never threaten liberty.

The Constitution imposes certain restrictions on the Congress designed to protect individual liberties, but unless the courts are independent and have the power to declare laws in violation of the Constitution null and void, those protections amount to nothing. The power of the Supreme Court to declare laws unconstitutional leads some people to assume that the judicial branch will be superior to the legislative branch. Hamilton examines this argument, starting with the fact that only the Constitution is fundamental law. To argue that the Constitution is not superior to the laws suggest that the representatives of the people are superior to the people and that the Constitution is inferior to the government it gave birth to. The courts are the arbiters between the legislative branch and the people; the courts are to interpret the laws and prevent the legislative branch from exceeding the powers granted to it. The courts must not only place the Constitution higher than the laws passed by Congress, they must also place the intentions of the people ahead of the intentions of their representatives. This is not a matter of which branch is superior: it is simply to acknowledge that the people are superior to both. It is futile to argue that the court's decisions, in some instances, might interfere with the will of the legislature. People argue that it is the function of Congress, not the courts, to pass laws and formulate policy. This is true, but to interpret the laws and judge their constitutionality are the two special functions of the court. The fact that the courts are charged with determining what the law means does not suggest that they will be justified in substituting their will for that of the Congress.

The independence of the courts is also necessary to protect the rights of individuals against the destructive actions of factions. Certain designing men may influence the legislature to formulate policies and pass laws that violate the Constitution or individual rights. The fact that the people have the right to change or abolish their government if it becomes inconsistent with their happiness is not sufficient protection; in the first place, stability requires that such changes be orderly and constitutional. A government at the mercy of groups continually plotting its downfall would be in a deplorable situation. The only way citizens can feel their rights are secure is to know that the judicial branch protects them against the people, both in and outside government, who work against their interests.

Hamilton cites one other important reason for judges to have life tenure. In a free government there are bound to be many laws, some of them complex and contradictory. It takes many years to fully understand the meaning of these laws and a short term of office would discourage able and honest men from seeking an appointment to the courts; they would be reluctant to give up lucrative law practices to accept a temporary judicial appointment. Life tenure, modified by good behavior, is a superb device for assuring judicial independence and protection of individual rights.

Analysis

With a view toward creating a judiciary that would constitute a balance against Congress, the Convention provided for the independence of the courts from Congress. Hamilton opposes vesting supreme judicial power in a branch of the legislative body because this would verge upon a violation of that "excellent rule," the separation of powers. Besides, due to the propensity of legislative bodies to party division, there is "reason to fear that the pestilent breath of faction may poison the fountains of justice." Hamilton, therefore, praises the Constitution for establishing courts that are separated from Congress. He is pleased to note that to this organizational independence there is added a financial one.

Another factor contributing to the independence of the judiciary is the judges' right to hold office during good behavior. It is in connection with his advocacy of that "excellent barrier to the encroachments and oppressions of that reprehensive body," that "citadel of the public justice," that Hamilton pronounces judicial review as being part of the Constitution. Judicial review is another barrier against too much democracy. Exercised by state courts before the Federal Convention met, and taken for granted by the majority of the members of the Convention, as well as by the ratifying conventions in the states, judicial review is expounded by Hamilton as a doctrine reaching a climax and a conclusion in this Federalist paper.

Starting out from the premise that "a constitution is, in fact, and must be regarded by the judged, as a fundamental law," Hamilton considers judicial review as a means of preserving that constitution and, thereby, free government. To be more concrete, when Hamilton considers the judiciary both as a barrier to the encroachments and oppressions of the representative body and as the citadel of public justice, i.e., the citadel for the protection of the individual's life, liberty, and property, he states that judicial review means a curb on the legislature's encroachments upon individual rights. Parallel to every denial of legislative power in essay seventy-eight goes an assertion of vested rights. Note that the Supreme Court did not ultimately grant itself the explicit power of judicial review until the case Marbury v. Madison in 1803.

Although he considers a power-concentration in the legislature as despotism, Hamilton does not perceive a strong judiciary as a threat to free government. He admits that individual oppression may now and then proceed from the courts, but he is emphatic in adding that the general liberty of the people can never be endangered from that quarter. When the judge unites integrity with knowledge, power is in good hands. As the "bulwarks of a limited Constitution against legislative encroachments," they will use that power for the protection of the individual's rights rather than for infringements upon those rights.

Through judicial review vested rights are protected not only from the legislature, they are also protected from the executive. An executive act that is sanctioned by the courts and –– since it is the duty of the judges to declare void legislative acts contrary to the Constitution –– that is thus in conformity with the will of the people as laid down in the Constitution, cannot be an act of oppression.

Summary and Analysis of Essay 79

Summary

Hamilton continues where he left off, claiming that next to permanency in office "nothing can contribute more to independence of the judges than a fixed provision of support." Hamilton argues that a power over a man's living is a power over his will, and therefore by removing this temptation, you once again strengthen the power of the judiciary. You cannot let the judiciary depend on the legislature for pensions because that destroys the separation between the two branches.

The Constitution proves that judges of the United States "shall at stated times receive for their services a compensation which shall not be diminished during their continuance in office." The legislature is able to increase the amount of money at times (because of inflation) but cannot decrease the money, and therefore, does not have power to influence a judge and the separation of powers remains rigid.

The other important aspect of the judicial system is the "want of removing a judge." Hamilton believes, however, that more damage is done to liberty when you try to draw a line between inability and ability than when judges can be removed more easily. Age is also a silly consideration, because who can say when someone can no longer facilitate, and learning the laws of the land is a difficult and life-long task.

Analysis

While Hamilton mentions many of the strengths of the judiciary in this short Federalist Paper, many of the strengths of the judiciary process under the Constitution are implied and not as explicit as Hamilton laid out in this essay. Like the amending process, judicial review can adjust the Constitution to new conditions. Although the Federalist does not make a direct statement on that function of the judges, such a function can be concluded from other remarks.

The Constitution is, according to the authors, supposed to last for generations. Consequently the judges, being the "guardians of the Constitution," will have to interpret the law with a view to preserving it. This means that they will have to interpret it in a manner that takes into account changed conditions that might exist in new environments and times. Chief Justice Marshall's later dictum, "We must never forget, that it is a constitution we are expounding, ... a constitution intended to endure for ages to come, and , consequently, to be adopted to the various crises of human affairs" - a statement largely of judicial guardianship of the Constitution by means of adjustment, as suggested in The Federalist Papers.

The supremacy of the Constitution over the people furnishes us with an indication of the importance of the judiciary. As the natural -- and only -- interpreters of the law, the judges, while being bound by the Constitution, are not bound by the will of the people, unless that will has become part of the Constitution. They thereby occupy that peculiar position assigned to them in the Federalist, being, of all people, closest to the Constitution and its revelations of justice. The judges, being bound by the Constitution, are also bound by certain principles of higher law of which the Constitution is a reflection. The Federalist indicates that the Constitution is not only the source, but also the recipient of superior law: although Hamilton says that "by a limited constitution, I understand one which contains certain specific exceptions to the legislative authority," his use of the term "limited" instead of "limiting" suggests also that the Constitution itself is limited by certain principles that secure the protection of the states and the rights of the individual, and that constitutional restrictions upon the legislative and amending power are only expressions of those higher law principles that rule the Constitution. The judges thus are the guardians not only of the letter but also of the spirit of the Constitution. This makes them truly platonic guardians who, while not being unwilling to take into account new conditions that may arise in the course of time, guarantee the preservation of the values of the Constitution and thus secure justice, which is refereed to in the Federalist as the end of government.

Summary and Analysis of Essay 80

Summary

Hamilton introduces five principles of federal judiciary authority and then demonstrates how the proposed constitution conforms to them. Specifically, the principles describe what kinds of cases federal courts ought to have jurisdiction over. Madison contends that the federal judiciary ought to decide cases that

1) relate federal laws,

2) relate to the US Constitution,

3) involve the US government as a party in the case,

4) affect the "peace of the confederacy," and

5) involve maritime disputes.

Hamilton defends the need for federal judicial authority over cases involving federal laws by arguing that the laws would not be followed if the government did not have the power to enforce them. He furthermore argues that it is necessary for judicial power to be "coextensive" with the legislature in order to ensure "uniformity in the interpretation of national laws." If each state had its own court of final jurisdiction, then "nothing but contradiction and confusion can proceed." Hamilton also argues that the federal judiciary must have jurisdiction over cases that could lead to war since "the peace of the whole ought not to be left at the disposal of a part." That is, the entire country should not be at risk of war as the result of a decision made by a particular state's court.

Having established the basic principles guiding the proper extent of judicial authority, Hamilton then shows how the specific provisions of the constitution relating to the judiciary conform to these principles. He responds to objections to the federal judiciary having authority over issues of "equity," i.e. loans and financial obligations, by arguing that it is very likely for such cases to arise and involve either multiple states or foreigners, thus making necessary federal jurisdiction.

Analysis

This paper continues The Federalist's extended discussion of the judiciary by discussing the specific areas in which the federal courts will have final authority. The question of federal court jurisdiction was very contentious during the debate over the constitution. Anti-Federalists feared that national courts would abridge the rights of the states and become a tool of tyrants. These opponents argued that local courts were safer than national ones.

Hamilton buttresses his argument with the example of pre-modern Germany: "History gives us a horrid picture of the dissentions and private wars which distracted and desolated Germany, prior to the institution of the Imperial Chamber by Maximillian, towards the close of the fifteenth century; and informs us, at the same time, of the vast influence of that institution, in appeasing the disorders, and establishing the tranquility of the empire. This was a court invested with authority to decide finally all differences among the members of the Germanic body." This repeats a common strategy of the Federalist's authors, the use of historical examples to justify a strong, energetic national government.

Summary and Analysis of Essay 81

Summary

Hamilton describes the separation of judicial authority among the different types of courts and the relationship between these courts. The part of the Constitution in question is Article 3, Section 1, which states, "The judicial power of the United States is to be vested in one supreme court, and in such inferior courts as the congress may from time to time ordain and establish."

Hamilton begins this paper by summarizing the anti-federalist critique of this constitutional provision. The anti-federalists feared that the supreme court would have the power to interpret laws passed by congress according to the "spirit" of the constitution. This would then lead to the court being able to "mould" laws passed by congress "into whatever shape it may think proper." Such a power would make the Supreme Court superior to the national legislature.

However, Hamilton argues that "there is not a syllable in the plan, which directly empowers the national courts to construe the laws according to the spirit of the constitution." That is, the federal courts will not have unlimited power to interpret laws as they see fit. Hamilton suggests further that the American people need not be concerned about the Supreme Court being separate from the legislature. He argues that the legislature, which makes the laws, cannot be trusted to interpret the laws impartially: "From a body which had had even a partial agency in passing bad laws, we could rarely expect a disposition to temper and moderate them in the application." Furthermore, legislators are unlikely to have the same level of legal expertise as a distinct body of magistrates would. Finally, the legislature is liable to be divided by political factions, making it even less likely that it will act impartially in deciding legal matters.

Hamilton argues further that the judiciary is a relatively weak branch of government and therefore poses very little threat to liberty. Unlike the other branches of government, the judiciary cannot "support its usurpations by force." All it can do is declare its judgment. Plus, the judges are themselves personally subject to impeachment and removal from office by the legislature.

Hamilton then discusses the creation of inferior federal courts. It had been objected that state courts could perform this function; however, Hamilton contends that "a local spirit" may bias the opinions of state judges.

Hamilton also clarifies which cases will fall under the Supreme Court's "original jurisdiction," i.e. the cases that must go directly to the Supreme Court to be decided. Such cases are limited to those "affecting ambassadors, other public ministers and consuls, and those in which a state shall be a party." Thus, in most instances, the Supreme Court will only be a court of appeals.

Finally, Hamilton addresses concerns that the Supreme Court's role as an appellate court will abolish the trial by jury. It had been feared that if the Supreme Court could hear appeals and base its decisions on the facts of the case, instead of just legal theory, then trial juries would essentially become powerless.

Analysis

This paper illuminates an interesting debate over the separation of powers. The anti-federalists were animated in large part by the fear that the proposed constitution would lead to the creation of an overly powerful central government that could eventually develop into a tyranny. The anti-federalists generally argued in favor of relatively strong state governments and a relatively weak federal government. One of the founders' strategies for addressing this concern of an overly powerful national government was the principle of separation of powers. In this paper, Hamilton discusses the importance of having a distinct federal court system completely independent of the legislature. This would allow for impartiality in the judicial system. However, the anti-federalists wanted the legislature to have judicial authority since the legislature would be composed of the direct representatives of the people and thus less likely to be tyrannical. However, Hamilton argues that if the judicial branch and legislative branch were combined, there would be a greater chance of bias and injustice.

Interestingly, the anti-federalists felt that the separation of powers in this particular case was a threat to liberty. They wanted the legislature to be supreme in all matters, including judicial ones. Whereas previously the anti-federalists had been concerned about an overly powerful national legislature, they argue in this case that the legislature is too weak. However, for Hamilton, the fundamental point is that the people who make the law cannot also be trusted to always apply the law impartially. If, for example, a particular law were unconstitutional, it could only be struck down if the same entity that passed the law admitted that it had made a grave error.

Summary and Analysis of Essay 82

Summary

Hamilton addresses concerns that the proposed constitution would deprive state judicial systems of their authority. Hamilton argues that the states will "retain all pre-existing authorities which may not be exclusively delegated to the federal head." That is, the default is that state courts will have the same powers under the proposed constitution as they did under the Articles. It is only particular powers, explicitly listed in the Constitution, that are granted solely to the federal government and denied to the states.

Hamilton furthermore discusses the doctrine of "concurrent jurisdiction," i.e. legal cases that both federal courts and state courts have the authority to decide. Essentially, unless a case falls into a category specifically listed in the Constitution as falling under the sole authority of the national courts, all cases fall under the jurisdiction of the state courts. The only power the federal courts have over the states is the power of appeal; that is, citizens can appeal state court decisions to federal courts.

Hamilton stresses throughout this paper the importance of conceiving of the state and federal courts as part of "one whole." The Constitution sought to create a coherent legal system that would ensure laws would be enforced uniformly throughout the country. Thus, the Constitution would not take away the powers of the state courts, as the anti-federalists feared, but rather integrate them into a cohesive national system.

Analysis

One of the central arguments of the anti-federalists was that the proposed constitution would undermine the authority of the state courts: "The Judiciary of the Unite States is so constructed and extended, as to absorb and destroy the judiciaries of the several States; thereby rendering law as tedious, intricate and expensive, and justice as unattainable, by a great part of the community, as in England, and enabling the rich to oppress and ruin the poor" (Mason 174). The state courts were seen as less of a threat to the liberty and rights of the people than federal courts.

Hamilton addresses this concern by painting a picture of a cohesive, harmonious judicial system that gives state courts a specific role within the national system of government. He contends that state courts will retain most of their powers. Only in specific, limited respects does the proposed constitution deny jurisdiction to state judiciaries.

Summary and Analysis of Essay 83

Summary

In this final paper on the judiciary, and the longest paper in the Federalist, Hamilton responds to concerns about the absence of a constitutional provision for trial by jury in civil cases. Although the Constitution explicitly protects the right to trial by jury in criminal cases, it does not offer such a guarantee in civil cases (e.g. law suits). Anti-federalists argued that this omission was a deliberate attempt to deny citizens the right to a jury trial in civil cases.

Hamilton responds that just because the Constitution does not specifically guarantee the right to trial by jury in civil cases does not mean that juries are forbidden in such cases. Rather, the Constitution leaves it to the national legislature to decide whether to allow for juries in civil cases and even to specify in what kinds of civil cases juries may be allowed. Hamilton argues that it was necessary to specifically guarantee the right to trial by jury in criminal cases since judicial malpractice in such cases poses a far greater threat to the liberty of the individual than civil cases. It was widely believed that juries could be trusted more than individual judges to uphold justice. Thus, in cases where the verdict may result in the accused facing prison time or execution, it is essential that juries be allowed.

Civil cases, in contrast, do not threaten the existence of liberty in the same way. Hamilton argues further that civil cases are far more complicated and varied than criminal cases, so much so that they may be beyond the ability of the average citizen serving on a jury to comprehend. In civil cases involving complex financial transactions and business disputes, the minute details may be beyond the ability of average citizens to judge fairly. Other cases, such as those involving disputes with other nations, could also be inappropriate for juries since they may involve highly sensitive issues that, if not handled delicately, might lead to war.

Hamilton concludes, therefore, that it is best left to Congress to determine when juries should be allowed in civil cases. The authors of the Constitution did not intend to abolish trial by jury in civil cases. Rather, they thought it prudent to leave it to the representatives of the people to decide in which types of civil cases juries should be allowed.

Analysis

This paper illustrates once again the widespread concern in the early days of the American republic about guarding personal liberty against the usurpations of an overly powerful government. Hamilton's attempts to dismiss concerns over the absence of a specific constitutional provision for trial by jury in civil cases are rooted in one of the core principles of constitutional theory: the general "genius" of government is more effective than "particular provisions." Using examples from

Europe and the several states, Hamilton shows that specifically dictating that juries must be allowed in civil cases would lead to inefficiency and miscarriages of justice due to the wide variety and considerable complexity in civil law. Opponents of the constitution wanted specific guarantees of the right to trial by jury in civil cases; however, Hamilton sees this as better left to the national legislature.

This paper therefore shows the attempts by the founders to give the Constitution as much flexibility as possible. The founders did not want to overly restrict the future actions of the national legislature with constitutional provisions on minute matters. The purpose of the Constitution is to provide a general framework for government in the United States, not a detailed and comprehensive set of laws. Issues such as the mode of trial in civil cases fall into the category of details best decided by the representatives of the people.

Summary and Analysis of Essay 84

Summary

Hamilton begins the penultimate Federalist paper by acknowledging that there are some objections to the Constitution that have not yet been discussed. The most important of the remaining objections is that the Constitution does not contain a bill of rights. It has already been pointed out that several state constitutions do not contain bills of rights, including New York State. Oddly, New York citizens who oppose the federal constitution on the ground that it does into contain a bill of rights have tremendous admiration for their state constitution. These citizens claim that the state constitution does not need a separate bill of rights because the guarantee of individual rights is written into the constitution itself. The same is true of the federal constitution.

As was previously shown, many safeguards against the abuse of power are built into the structure of the national government, such as the separation of powers and checks and balances. In this paper, Hamilton contends that he will examine six provisions designed to protect individual liberties. First, to protect the people against executive and judicial abuse of power, the Constitution provides the power to impeach. Second, the writ of habeas corpus (the right of a person arrested to imprisoned to be informed of the charges against him) shall not be suspended, "unless, when in cases of rebellion or invasion the public safety may require it." Next, Bills of attainder and ex-post-facto laws are prohibited. The great English jurist, Blackstone, believed that prohibiting these types of laws were the two most fundamental individual rights. Fourth, the Constitution states "no title of nobility should be granted by the United States." Hamilton writes that the importance of prohibiting titles of nobility is paramount; if such titles were granted, the very foundation of republican government would be undermined. Fifth, the Constitution guarantees the right to trial by jury in all criminal cases and sixth, treason is very carefully defined in the Constitution. The Constitution supports the distinction between political dissent and treason, it does all it can to prevent working a hardship on the traitor's family.

Originally, bills of rights were agreements between kings and their subjects concerning the rights of the people. Kings limited their own power, either under pressure or voluntarily, acknowledging that they were not all-powerful. The best example is the Magna Carta, the charter of English liberties that the barons forcibly obtained from King John in 1215. But one must remember that the proposed Constitution has no force unless the people approve it; there is no need to grant them specific rights. The Preamble of the Constitution is a better recognition of popular rights than all the bills of rights put together. The Constitution is concerned with general political interest and rights, not with specific and minute details of every right. Hamilton argues that a bill of rights would not only be unnecessary, but dangerous. A bill of rights would, for instance, attempt to limit certain governmental powers which are not even granted.

Another objection to the Constitution is that the national government will be so far away from the states and the people that the latter will be ignorant of what is going on. The counties in opposition to state governments can make the same argument. There are ways of knowing what the state governments are up to, just as there are ways of knowing what is happening in the nation's capitol; we can evaluate the laws that are passed, correspond with our representatives, read newspaper reports, etc. If this were not so, there would be no division of governmental power whatsoever in a republican form of government. Not only will the people be able to take stock of the national government, the states will act as sentinels or guards; they will keep a watchful eye over all the branches of the national government. This is so because the state and national governments will be rivals for power. Actually, the people will be more fully informed concerning the conduct of their national representative than they are, at present, of the state representatives.

There are many curious and extraordinary objections to the Constitution, but one of the strangest, this paper suggests, has to do with debts owed by the states to the United States. Some people have gone so far as to suggest that the Constitution removes the obligations of the states to pay their debts. This claim is ridiculous. Last, there has been an objection concerning the expense of the proposed government. When we consider that most Americans are convinced that Union is vital to their political happiness, that is cannot be preserved under the present system, that new and broad powers ought to be granted to the national government, the question of added dispense seems superficial. Good government is far too important to allow expense to interfere. Undeniably, there will be some added expense, but there will be some savings as well. All in all, Hamilton believes that this is an extremely weak argument.

Analysis

It is extremely interesting and telling that Hamilton wrote this essay, not Madison, and shows the internal inconsistencies between the two authors. While Alexander Hamilton writes in this essay of the lack of a need for a Bill of Rights and argues not that the Constitution will eventually have the ideals that Americans presently feel our fundamental, but instead, that they are unnecessary and would actually be hurtful to the Constitution. That his coauthor was James Madison, considered the father of the Bill of Rights, is an ironic twist of fate and if Madison and not Hamilton had written this segment of the Federalist Papers, it would have been far different.

This paper also shows something on the nature of government that Hamilton desired. Free government being an ideal, Hamilton concedes that the plan of the convention is a compound as much as the errors and prejudices, as of the sense and wisdom, of the delegates, a compromise of many dissimilar interest and inclinations. It has not claim to absolute perfection. Not expecting "to see a perfect work from imperfect man," (Federalist 85), Hamilton has praise for the Constitution. The system it establishes, "thought it may not be perfect in every part, is, on the whole, a good one; it is the best that present views ad circumstances of the country will permit."

The entire change that was effected by the Constitution consists in the creation of the Union. Not being ratified, as were the Articles, merely by the "several legislatures," but "by the PEOPLE" of America, irrespective of state boundaries, the Constitution transforms a league under international law into a nation. More specifically, the radial alterations of the Articles of Confederation mean to Hamilton the grant of "new and extensive powers . . . to the national head, and . . . a different organization of the federal government – a single body being an unsafe depository of such ample authorities." The Constitution, while concentrating power in the federal head as a remedy against democratic tyranny in the states, diminishes the probability of too much democracy on the national level by taking power away from Congress. The achievement of free government in the Constitution thus boils down to a restriction of popular government in favor of the protection of the individual's rights. It is brought about mainly by two factors: the creation of a stronger national government and the dethronement of an all-powerful legislature.

Summary and Analysis of Essay 85

Summary

In this concluding Federalist Paper, Hamilton begins by telling his readers that he will not discuss the remaining two points in his outline, "the analogy of the proposed governments to the states," and "the additional security which this adoption will afford to republican government, to liberty, and to property," because he has already said all that he has to about these subjects.

He continues that the Constitution has much in similar to the New York state government, especially in consideration of its defects, including the ability of the president to be reelected, "the want of a council, the omission of a formal bill of rights, and the omission of a provision respecting the liberty of the press." It is ironic that the strongest opponents of the Constitution say that they are happy with the laws of their state, especially because its Constitution contains the same vulnerabilities.

Hamilton proceeds to ask the rhetorical question of whether or not the Constitution has been vindicated from the critic's attacks. Although each man must ask this for himself, Hamilton believes that this duty must be taken extremely seriously, because there will be no excuse for the wrong decision, a vote that has grave consequences for the future of the nation. He heeds the individual man to remember not only the magnitude of the decision, but also the fact that the majority of the nation has already approved the Constitution.

Continuing, Hamilton admits, "Concessions on the part of the friends of the plan, that it has not a claim to absolute perfection, have afforded matter of no small triumph." They ask why they should not make the Constitution perfect before it is adopted. Hamilton answers this critique by claiming that no one can be found who does not believe that the "system is good," and that delay is useless and will only prolong the precarious situation of the nation. In addition, Hamilton contends "I never hope to see a perfect work for imperfect men." It is improbable to have another convention, but Hamilton believes that the subject of amendments has yet to be considered in The Federalist Papers. Hamilton believes that future amendments will be much easier to obtain than changing the Constitution. Amendments, unlike the Constitution itself, will be easier to pass because no compromise or negotiation will be necessary because it will be a singular proposition and not a whole document, like the Constitution.

Hamilton concludes by quoting David Hume, "to balance a large state or society, whether monarchial or republican, on general laws, is a work of so great difficulty that no human genius, however comprehensive, is able, by the mere dint of reason and reflection, to effect it. The judgments of many must united in the work; experience must guide their labor; time must bring it to perfection, and the feeling of inconveniences must correct the mistakes which they inevitably fall into their first trials and experiments." Hamilton concludes strongly, saying, "a country without a national government is, in my view, an awful spectacle." On the other hand, a Constitution, established by the people, "is a prodigy," something that he looks forward to with "trembling anxiety." He dreads the consequences of new attempts because men and states are enemies to national governments in every state.

Analysis

The Constitution is, on the one hand, lauded by the authors for providing for amendments. On the other hand, it is praised for making the amending process a rather rigid one. In the last number of the Federalist, Hamilton notes that the Constitution, once it is adopted, can be amended. He stressed that, whereas the ratification of the Constitution requires the assent of all the states, subsequent amendments would require only the consent of three-fourths of the members of the Union, happily concluding that there can be "no comparison between the facility of affecting an amendment, and that of establishing in the first instance a complete Constitution." Answering the argument that the national government might prevent amendments, the New Yorker emphasizes that "the intrinsic difficulty of governing thirteen States . . .will. .. constantly impose on the national rulers the necessity of a spirit of accommodation to the reasonable expectations of their constituents." Whenever two-thirds of the states concur, Congress will be obliged to call a convention for proposing amendments, which shall be valid when ratified by the legislatures of 3/4 of the states or by conventions of 3/4 thereof. Although it may be difficult to muster the required majority for amendments that merely affect local interests, there can be no doubt that the situation would be different in the case of amendments concerning "the general liberty and security of the people." Hamilton concludes by saying that Americans may, as far as their rights are concerned, "safely rely on the disposition of the State legislatures to erect barriers against the encroachments of the national government."

While expressing satisfaction about the possibility of change, consider the provisions concerning amendment as a bulwark for the preservation of fundamental values that are deemed necessary for a free government, name, the rights of the states, and the freedom of the individual. It appears that in their discussions, states' rights stand in the foreground. Hamilton discusses them at great length, and Madison mentions nothing but states' rights. However, this should not blind us to the fact that to both authors the preservation of those rights also amounts to a preservation of individual freedom. We know that Madison, in his essays, conceives of the states as playing an important role in the protection of the individual. Therefore, when he praises the Constitution for perpetuating the 'residuary sovereignty' of the states, he need not, in so many words, stress the relevance of that sovereignty for the protection of the freedom of the individual, because that relevance is implicit. On the other hand, Hamilton, who in the Federalist pronounces a doctrine of happiness through national power, has to put greater emphasis on the importance of the states for the protection of individual's rights. Consequently, when remarking on the amending process, he expressly relates the states to "the general liberty and security of the people." We may thus say that the Federalist , in commenting on amendments, points to the usefulness of the amending process to the preservation of the freedom and the individual.

In conclusion, the Federalist does not give a precise answer as to the nature of the union. With respect to the establishment of the new system, Madison states in so many words that the constituents' act is a contract between the sovereign states. Still, when he refers to those who ratify the Constitution as "the American people," he creates doubts as to whether in substance, ratification might not be an expression of the will of the nation, in spite of the fact that in form it would definitely be an act of the people of the various states. Hamilton's statements seem to be even more ambiguous. Strangely enough, the prophet of the nationalists does not even use the term "the American people" in his comments on ratification. When he writes that the people will ratify the Constitution, he -— unlike Madison —- refrains from saying whether he means the people of the states or the nation, a peculiar omission from an advocate of the nationalist doctrine. If the author's comments on the substance of the Constitution are considered, a similar ambiguity as to the nature of the Union is apparent.

This ambiguity makes the Federalist a genuine equivalent of the Constitution it interprets. In Philadelphia, Madison stated that the Convention was not confronted with "two extremes," namely, " a perfect separation and a perfect incorporation of the thirteen States." The same can be said of the authors of the Federalist. In this work Hamilton, who appears definitely as the greater nationalist, declares himself to be as little in favor of a perfect incorporation of the thirteen states as Madison, the champion of states' rights, is of a perfect separation of the states. The Constitution being a "bundle of compromises," it seems only natural if its classic commentary, the Federalist, refrains from committing itself on the nature of that law's greatest compromise, the Union. In the last number of the Federalist there can be found a reaffirmation of the idea that the Constitution is a compromise and that there is no clear-cut answer to the nature of the Union it establishes. As if he wanted to assure both the nationalists and the advocates of states' rights alike that the Constitution and its Union offered some common ground for them to meet, Hamilton states that "the compacts which are to embrace thirteen distinct States in a common bond of amity and union, must as necessarily be a compromise of as many dissimilar interests and inclinations. How can perfection spring from such materials?" Thus the man who, throughout his essays, had given a highly nationalistic version of the Constitution, in the end not only admits that the more perfect Union would come into existence through a compact, but even goes so far as to say that it would be created through a whole number of compacts --— a clear concession to the states' rights concept of a contract theory of the nature of the Union!

Suggested Essay Questions

1. According to the authors of the Federalist Papers, what was the key failure of the Articles of Confederation?

   The fundamental weakness of the Articles, according to the authors of the Federalist Papers, was that they did not give the national government the power to enforce its decrees on the member states. The national government could levy taxes on the states or require them to contribute a certain number of soldiers to the national force, but the government had no way of punishing states that did not comply. As a result, the decrees of the national government were authoritative orders on paper, but in fact were mere requests. Essentially, the state governments were stronger than the national government, making it impossible for the latter to govern effectively.

2. Why were the provisions in the Constitution regarding the American military so controversial?

   There is a long Anglo-American tradition of fear of standing armies, professional forces that serve during peacetime. It was widely believed that standing armies gave the government the ability to forcefully usurp power and violate the rights and liberties of the people. Standing armies stood in sharp contrast to militias, which were military forces made up of local volunteers who only served during times of war. Militias fit into the republican ideal of citizens defending their own land and freedom. Militias were thought to inspire and nurture republican virtues of independence and liberty, whereas standing armies were thought to make citizens overly dependent on professional soldiers.

   The Constitution enabled Congress to raise and maintain a professional military force to be commanded by the President. Anti-Federalists feared that these provisions would enable the executive and legislative branches of government to conspire against the people and establish a tyrannical government.

3. What branch of government was accused of being aristocratic? Why?

   Many anti-federalists argued that the Senate would become an American aristocracy. In the original, unamended Constitution, Senators were to be elected by the state legislatures rather than directly by the people. This, combined with senatorial powers over presidential appointments to the executive and judiciary branch and treaties with foreign powers, led many to fear that the relatively small Senate would have excessive powers. Having just fought a war for independence from aristocratic England, Americans were keen to avoid recreating an aristocracy of their own.

4. What branch of government was accused of being monarchical? Why?

The executive branch, and the President specifically, was often derided by anti-federalists as an American king. Anti-federalists argued that, as commander-in-chief, the President would have sufficient power at his disposal to usurp power from the other branches of government and become a tyrant. Furthermore, the president's power to appoint public officials and judges was seen as a potential source of corruption. Anti-federalists also disliked the President's ability to veto legislation passed by Congress, since this was seen as undermining the authority of the direct representatives of the people.

5. According to the Federalist Papers, what is wrong with direct democracy?

In a direct democracy, citizens gather together in a public place and vote on public policy. They do not elect representatives to decide matters on their behalf, but make all political decisions themselves as one collective political entity. As Madison argues in paper 10, direct democracies are often swayed by temporary passions and frenzies. This leads to instability as the democratic society rapidly shifts policy one way or the other when a new idea becomes popular. It also leads to a violation of the rights of minorities since there is nothing to check the power of the majority. If even just 50.001% of the country, for example, supports going to war, the nation goes to war no matter how disastrous that decision might be.

6. According to the Federalist papers, what is the difference between a democracy and a republic?

In a democracy, all members of society gather together and administer the government in person. In a republic, citizens elect representatives to decide public matters on their behalf. According to Madison in paper 10, republican government is far superior to democracy for two reasons. First, by delegating authority to representatives, republican government ensures that "the public views" are reined and enlarged. It was thought that the elected representatives would be wiser and more virtuous than the great body of citizens and thus capable of making better decisions. Second, a republic allows for the government to extend over a large swath of territory. In a democracy, all citizens need to gather in one place to make decisions. It would clearly be impossible for all the citizens of the US to meet in Washington, D.C., and vote on public policy. However, it is very practical for a few representatives from each state to meet and make decisions. Having a larger republic means that the representatives will be chosen from a larger number of people, thus increasing the likelihood that the elected representatives will be good, virtuous people. Also, having many representatives in government helps guard against, as Madison writes, "the cabals of a few."

7. Define Federalism and explain its role in the American system of government.

Federalism is the sharing of power between the state governments and the national (or "Federal") government. In the American system of government, certain powers are exercised by only state governments or the federal government, while other powers are exercised by both. For example, only the federal government can make treaties with foreign powers or declare war, and only state governments can appoint officers in the militia. However, both the state and federal governments can levy taxes.

8. According to the Federalist papers, what advantages did state governments have over the national government?

The authors of the Federalist papers believed that the state governments would enjoy more support from the public than the federal government would. State officials would be closer to the people and have a more direct and obvious impact on their lives. In contrast, the federal government would be relatively distant and alien and thus less in-tune with the people. In any hypothetical conflict between the state and federal governments, the former would have a significant advantage due to the support of the people.

9. How does the principle of checks and balances influence the constitutional process for appointing public officials?

The founders were deeply concerned about one branch of government becoming significantly more powerful than the others. To prevent this, they created checks and balances that would enable each branch to the limit the powers of the others. In the case of official appointments, the President has the power to nominate officials, but the Senate must vote to approve these appointments. Thus, power over the appointment of public officials is shared between the executive and legislative branches of government. The clause requiring senatorial consent for presidential appointees serves as a check on the power of the president.

10. Why did the authors of the Federalist Papers fear the influence of factions?

The authors of the Federalist Papers believed that in any democratic or republican system of government, there was always a significant risk of certain segments of the population forming distinct interest groups. It was feared that these groups, or factions, would prioritize their own particular goals over the good of the nation. Due in part to the natural disinclination among people to admit their own mistakes or sacrifice their own interests, it was feared that factions would hinder the public policy-making process and hamstring the workings of government. The authors of the Federalist papers longed for virtuous political leaders who would act wisely and in the best interest of the country. However, they knew from experience and from their study of history that people tend to form factions and prioritize the faction's interest over the greater good.

Soldiers and Liberty: The Debate Over Standing Armies and Militias in Early America

A 2009 Gallup Poll of American adults revealed broad public support for the American military. With over 80% of respondents reporting "a great deal" or "quite a lot" of confidence in the American military, America's armed forces today enjoy more support than any other major national institution.

This was not always the case. In the early years of American independence, as statesmen debated the form American government should take, the role of the military was a hotly contested issue. One of the several powers granted Congress in Article I of the US Constitution is to "raise and support armies" and to "provide for organizing, arming, and disciplining, the Militia, and for governing such Part of them as may be employed in the Service of the United States." Article II provided that the President would be the Commander in Chief of these forces. These provisions, granting the national government ultimate responsibility for the nation's defense, infuriated the Anti-Federalists, who saw such an arrangement as an usurpation of states' rights and a threat to American liberty. The Federalists responded, with equal vigor, that such provisions were essential to the security of the American Republic.

This paper examines both the convictions that informed opposition to national military forces and the arguments used to defend the Constitution's provisions for such forces. In opposing the powers over national military forces granted to the President and Congress by the Constitution, the Anti-Federalists were operating within an established Anglo-American tradition of mistrust for standing armies. The fear of standing armies as a fundamental threat to liberty was based on two convictions. First, standing armies were alien to the basic social and political structure of the English Constitution and, consequently, in possession of an inherent interest to overthrow it through either direct usurpation of authority or support for a tyrant. Second, at the time standing armies consisted of the morally degenerate dregs of society and were a corrupting influence on the rest of the population. In short, standing armies were antithetical to the ideals of limited, constitutional monarchy. They were a powerful and dangerous institution that did not fit within the framework of limited powers and did not conform to the principle of a free citizenry. Such arguments had tremendous influence on American conceptions of republican government and provided the basis of the Anti-Federalists' opposition to the proposed Constitution's provisions for national defense. The Anti-Federalists viewed the national government's power to raise and command a standing army in peacetime and to exert control over state militias as a dangerous step in the direction of arbitrary, monarchical government. The Anti-Federalists furthermore contended that standing armies and a nationally controlled militia threatened the republican character of the American people. Like their English predecessors, the Anti-Federalists saw standing armies as a source of moral corruption that would weaken the spirit of independence and liberty that was the foundation of America's martial strength.

In defending the Constitution's provisions for a standing army and national control of state militias, The Federalist does not depart from the traditional republican fears expressed above. Although it contends that a standing army and centrally controlled militia are necessary, The Federalist nevertheless sees them as a necessary evil, not a moral good. Rather than question the Anti-Federalists' fear of standing armies, The Federalist leverages it in defense of a political structure that will reduce the need for such forces and, to the extent they must exist, prevent them from threatening American liberty. Rather than question the Anti-Federalists' view of standing armies as morally degenerate and incompatible with the American spirit, The Federalist's defense of the national government's military powers implies a faith in the ability of the American people to resist any usurpation of power by a national military.

This paper will proceed in three parts. First, an analysis of writings by John Trenchard from the late 17th century, a series of orations delivered in Boston following the Boston Massacre of 1770, and an American anti-military tract from 1783, will introduce traditional Anglo-American views of standing armies and militias. The paper will then show how the Anti-Federalists adopted much of the same arguments in their opposition to the proposed Constitution. An interpretation of The Federalist's response to these arguments will then demonstrate how the proponents of the Constitution reconciled fears of national military forces with the republican character of the proposed political system.

Opposition to standing armies in English political thought was based in part on the belief that such forces existed outside the traditional social and political structure on which the English Constitution depended. As John Trenchard argued, the Constitution depended on "a due balance between king, lords, and commons" and on "the mutual occasions and necessities they have of one another." In order to preserve this balance, it was essential that the armed forces charged with defending the nation reflect this natural distribution of power: "…this balance can never be preserved but by an union of the natural and artificial strength of the kingdom, that is, by making the militia to consist of the same persons as have the property." If the army's structure reflected the balance of power in society—i.e. with the king as general, the lords as great commanders, and the freeholders as the rank and file—it would be "almost impossible" for such a force to "act to the disadvantage of the Constitution" since they would have no incentive to do so. Unlike soldiers in a standing army, who had "nothing to lose" and no "other tie to engage their fidelity, than the inconsiderable pay of six-pence a day, which they may have from the conqueror," the members of the militia had an inherent interest in upholding the Constitution: "Why may not the nobility, gentry, and free-holders of England be trusted with the defense of their own lives, estates and liberties, without having guardians and keepers assign'd them?" An attack on the Constitution would be an attack on their own interests. As John Hancock would argue almost a century later in 1774, "from a well regulated militia we have nothing to fear; their interest is the same with that of the state." Put simply, militias have estates to protect while standing armies have estates to get.

English and American opponents of standing armies held that, as institutions existing outside the normal balance of power, these forces would possess limitless power. Even if Parliament were given nominal control over a standing army, the soldiers could easily intimidate the elected representatives of the people: "...we very well know their [the Army's] desires are always commands..." and "...there is no debating nor disputing against legions." It was feared that once a standing army were permitted to exist, its power would be absolute. Attempts to limit the influence of soldiers by controlling their funding would be in vain: "We cannot buy it off for two very good Reasons: No Money will be taken for it; and we shall have nothing to give which is not theirs already: Our Estates, Lives and Liberties will be all at their command. They will have the Keys of our Money, and the Titles to our Lands in their tower." Even if the Army did not take power for itself, a King could nevertheless use it to seize absolute authority: "'The King has an Army,' stops all Mouths and cuts off all Reply. It is as if it should be said, 'Set your hearts at rest, for the King has all Power in his hands, and you have none: He has all your Estates, Lives and Liberties, under his Girdle: Slaves, and talk!'" Thus, the existence of a standing army was seen as an inherent threat to English liberty. A power so great would eliminate any need the King had for Parliament and consequently prevent the latter from checking the power of the former.

Opposition to standing armies was further influenced by the notion that professional soldiers were morally degenerate beings whose character was incompatible with the ideals of independence and virtue. Defined by their violent profession, interested only in fortune, and devoid of any virtue or higher moral principles, soldiers were a source of corruption threatening the virtues that were deemed critical to the survival of liberty. Trenchard saw soldiers as "men of dissolute and debauched principles" who care nothing for justice and are motivated by money alone. Such men "must be false, rapacious and cruel in their own defense. For having no other profession or subsistence to depend upon, they are forced to stir up the ambition of princes...that they may share of the spoils they make." The character of the soldier was furthermore equated to that of slaves. This made them particularly dangerous "in the midst of a free nation" since "slaves envy the freedom of others and take a malicious pleasure in contributing to destroy it." Rather than engage in debate to resolve disputes and make independent decisions as free and equal citizens, soldiers are "taught to consider arms as the only arbiters by which every dispute is to be decided." They are accustomed to obeying the orders of their commanders "without inquiring into the justice of the cause they are engaged to support" and thus become "the ready engines of tyranny and oppression." Soldiers engaged in a "loose idle life" rather than a "laborious way of living." As John Hancock argued, they were oftentimes persons "unfit to live in civil societies, who have no other motives of conduct than those which a desire to present gratification of their passions suggests." They were murderers, thieves, quarrelers and womanizers, men who had "lost or given up their own liberties, and envy those who enjoy liberty." They had no values, no moral foundation, and would even, "for the addition of one penny a day to their wages...desert from the Christian cross and fight under the crescent of the Turkish Sultan." In short, these were "lawless" men who despised "the just restraints of civil authority" and thus threatened the moral foundation of society. When placed in cities, standing armies would quickly effect a corruption of morals on the population: "no vestige of freedom can remain in a state where such a force exists...the morals of the people will be gradually corrupted...they will contract such an habit of tame submission, as to become an easy prey to the brutal tyrant who rules them." Standing armies would quell the people's spirit of liberty and fright them into submission, with youth in particular being corrupted through interaction with the troops.

Having thus rejected standing armies, English advocates of constitutional monarchy and American republicans placed their faith in a militia composed of virtuous citizens as an enduring source martial strength. Militiamen do not fight for pecuniary gain or the ambition of a tyrant but for the preservation of their freedom and everything they hold dear:

> When a country is invaded, the militia are ready to appear in its defense; they march into the field with that fortitude which a consciousness of the justice of their cause inspires; they do not jeopardize their lives for a master who considers them only as the instruments of his ambition, and whom they regard only as the daily dispenser of the scanty pittance of bread and water. No, they fight for their houses, their lands, for their wives, their children, for all who claim the tenderest names, and are held dearest in their hearts, they fight ...for their liberty, and for themselves, and for their God..."

Unlike soldiers in a standing army, militiamen fought as free men. In fighting, each man exercised his individual will as a citizen rather than serve as the instrument of a tyrant's ambition. Militiamen fought, not to deprive others of liberty and property, but to protect their own and that of their neighbors. The strength of this force came from the virtue of the society it protected. An American anti-military tract published in 1783 drew an explicit link between the martial virtue of the American militia during the War of Independence and the virtue of American society at the outset of the conflict:

> This military virtue of our citizens: their sense of dignity, and contempt of danger; the gallant efforts they made; was not this, I say, the offspring of the equality and independent temper of men, who fought for themselves, and not for masters; and whose spirit was not trammeled or broken down by the oppression of an insolent nobility? This was that warm animating pride which disdained to look up to any human creature as a superior, which raised us armies, and fought campaigns without pay or covering...

Unlike standing armies, those who fought with militias kept the character of citizens even as they did the work of soldiers. For the militiamen, fighting was not a profession or a path to fortune but their duty as citizens.

The Anglo-American fear of standing armies and admiration of militias provided the basis of the Anti-Federalists' opposition to the United States Constitution's provisions for national defense. Like earlier opponents of standing armies, the Anti-Federalists feared that a military force fundamentally separate from the people would inevitably threaten liberty and undermine the virtuous spirit that had won American independence from the grip of an English tyrant.

The Anti-Federalists viewed the national government's power to raise and command a standing army in peacetime and to exert control over state militias as a dangerous step in the direction of arbitrary government that would threaten the rights of states and the liberties of individual citizens. The argument over military powers was part of the larger debate on the proper balance of power between federal and state government. Patrick Henry argued that a "consolidated government" in possession of both a standing army and authority over state militias would leave the states and their citizens without the means of opposing tyranny: "Your arms wherewith you could defend yourselves are gone...Did you ever read of any revolution in any nation, brought about by the punishment of those in power, inflicted by those who had no power at all?" The hired soldiers of a standing army, "the engines of despotism," would be ready at all times to "execute the execrable commands of tyranny," and the people, having lost control over their militia to Congress, would be left without any defense: "Have we the means of resisting disciplined armies, when our only defense, the militia is put into the hands of Congress?...They [Congress] will therefore act as they think proper: All power will be in their own possession." Like the English republicans, the Anti-Federalists were concerned about the separation between military power and the people: "A standing army in the hands of a government placed so independent of the people, may be made a fatal instrument to overturn public liberties." Rather than rely on the martial strength of the people for defense, the constitution proposed to establish a force that would upset the country's balance of power and give one segment of the political structure—i.e. the national government—the ability to oppress the rest of society.

Not only would the general government have absolute authority over the states and the citizenry through their control of the army, but it would also have ample reason to exercise that authority. As the Philadelphia Minority argued, senators and representatives in the national government would be "independent of the sentiments and resentment of the people," and the administration would have "a greater interest in the government than in the community." These men would ultimately not be responsible to the people and, as a result, would not enjoy their active support and affection. Such an unpopular government could only execute its laws "by the aid of a numerous standing army," which could as easily be used to enforce good laws as to "wrest from the people their constitutional liberties." This military execution of the laws would "very soon destroy all elective governments in the country, produce anarchy, or establish despotism." The standing army and select militia brought under control of the national government would be the means by which the government extended its influence down to the individual citizen. They would be the collector of taxes, the instrument by which the Congress could expropriate the property of the people. Furthermore, a tyrant in possession of a standing army could order citizens "out in the militia to exercise, and to march when and where he pleases. His officers can wantonly inflict the most disgraceful punishment on a peaceable citizen, under pretense of disobedience, or the smallest neglect of militia duty." Thus, rather than draw its strength from the affections of the American people, the government under the proposed Constitution would be empowered by soldiers. The Anti-Federalists believed that liberty could be protected only by a strong populace, by a citizenry in possession of hard power. A standing army and centrally controlled militia threatened to deprive the people of that power, "render[ing] opposition vain" and leaving American liberty at the mercy of men who could not be held accountable for their actions.

The Anti-Federalists often expressed their opposition to standing armies and nationally-controlled militias in terms of monarchy, aristocracy and military dictatorship. The Anti-Federalist "Philadelphiensis" referred to the president as the "president general" and feared that an executive in command of an army would quickly make himself King and impose a "despotic monarchy." The people would be reduced to "subjects of a military king" with their representatives in Congress little more than aristocratic "sycophants and flatterers." Even if Congress and the President did not use the army "for the purposes of supporting themselves in any usurpations of power," there was nevertheless a "great hazard, that an army will subvert the forms of government, under whose authority they are raised, and establish one according to the pleasure of their leader." Drawing on the examples of Julius Caesar and Oliver Cromwell, the Anti-Federalists argued that a standing army could easily overturn "the constitutional powers of the government" and "dictate any form they please." The only restraint on a standing army would be the virtue of its leaders, and the Anti-Federalists held too dim a view of human nature to place much faith in this protection: "Are we so much better than the people of other ages and of other countries, that the same allurements of power and greatness, which led them aside from their duty, will have no influence upon men in our country?" The Anti-Federalists therefore saw the power of the army as an inherent source of instability in the government. Not only did they doubt the willingness of the President and Congress to refrain from using military force to impose tyranny, but they also questioned whether the government itself could restrain the ambitions of a powerful standing army.

Much of the concern over the future of American liberty was rooted in the Anti-Federalists' understanding of how the character of soldiers differed from that of citizens. In explaining why the Continental Army did not impose a military dictatorship following the War of Independence, the Anti-Federalist "Brutus" referenced these two distinct characters: "Fortunately indeed for this country, it had at the head of the army, a patriot as well as a general; and many of our principal officers, had not abandoned the characters of citizens, by assuming that of soldiers…" Soldiers were thought to be particularly susceptible to the temptations of power and greatness and could easily be led astray by the opportunity for personal gain. Unlike republican citizens who prided themselves on virtue, independence, and a laborious way of life, standing armies were generally composed of the "dregs of the people" with little connection to the rest of society: "As they are a body of men exempt from the common occupations of social life, having an interest different from the rest of the community, they wanton in the lap of ease and indolence, without feeling the duties, which arise from the political connection, though drawing their subsistence from the bosom of the state." Soldiers were seen as useless, lazy, inconvenient, and expensive burdens since they had "no object of employment," besides fighting, and no legitimate role in the political life of the state. Like earlier opponents of standing armies, the Anti-Federalists saw the interests of soldiers as existing in tension with those of the citizenry. Citizens valued peace, independence, and the freedom to enjoy the fruits of their labor. Soldiers, in contrast, knew only violence and lived off the labor of the people around them. Furthermore, soldiers' experiences in the army made them fundamentally unfit for republican citizenship: "The severity of discipline necessary to be observed reduces them to a degree of slavery; the unconditional submission to the commands of their superiors, to which they are bound, renders them the fit instruments of tyranny and oppression." The Anti-Federalists feared that the proposed Constitution would create a distinct group of men, set apart from the rest of the population, guided by a different set of values that did not place a premium on independence and equality, motivated by interests contrary to those of the rest of the community, and in possession of the means to pursue those interests violently. Soldiers were thus the antithesis of republican virtue. They were utterly incapable of being independent, liberty-loving, politically active citizens bound by a common set of interests and duties.

It was furthermore feared that the vices of a standing army would be a source of moral corruption undermining the virtue of republican society. The Anti-Federalists argued that virtue was a prerequisite of freedom and the foundation of both prosperity and a healthy constitution. However, Standing armies were by their very nature a threat to this virtue: "It will inevitably sow the seeds of corruption and depravity of manners. Indolence will increase, and with it crimes cannot but increase. The springs of honesty will gradually grow lax and chaste, and severe manners be succeeded by those that are dissolute and vicious. Where a standing army is kept up, virtue never thrives." Thus, opposition to standing armies was based on more than just concerns about limiting the power of the general government and preventing the rise of tyrants. Like the republicans before them, the Anti-Federalists feared standing armies would weaken the spirit of independence and liberty and destroy the republican virtue that was the ultimate source of America's martial strength. The Anti-Federalists argued that, rather than depend on a standing army, the United States should rely on the spirit of its people for defense "…Where is the danger? If, Sir, there was any, I would recur to the American spirit to defend us; that spirit which has enabled us to surmount the greatest difficulties." The Anti-Federalists understood liberty to be the foundation of the American spirit. It was the ultimate source of strength, one that could overcome any obstacle. The Anti-Federalists feared the consequences of affording such a powerful, prominent and proximate position to a group of men who were a threat to this liberty and the opposite of everything Republicanism stood for. In the imagination of the Anti-Federalists, it was Republican virtue that had triumphed over the British Army and guarded American liberty. Anything that threatened that virtue was intolerable.

In addition to the danger they posed, the Anti-Federalists believed standing armies were ultimately unnecessary. Patrick Henry argued that the defenders of the Constitution exaggerated the threats from Europe and the potential for domestic insurrections. While "Brutus" admitted a need for troops to guard certain outposts and for Congress to be able to raise armies in response to a threat, he thought entirely unnecessary a blanket provision enabling Congress to maintain armies in times of piece. Instead, he proposed authorizing Congress to raise armies in response to particular threats and exigencies.

Instead of standing armies and a centrally controlled militia, the Anti-Federalists preferred to entrust their security to state militias composed of and controlled by the people themselves. As Akhil Amar argues in his discussion of the 2nd Amendment, the "militia were the people and the people were the militia." What the Anti-Federalists wanted was a militia that would look like America, a fighting force composed of citizen-soldiers, men who were motivated by love of liberty and a desire to protect their homeland: "a well-regulated militia, duly trained to discipline…when it is necessary to embody an army…at once form a band of soldiers, whose interests are uniformly the same with those of the whole community, and in whose safety they see involved every thing that is dear to themselves." However, central control over state militias threatened to undermine the republican character of this force. Richard Henry Lee, for example, envisioned a scenario by which Congress could undermine the strength of "the yeomanry of the country" through its authority to organize the militia. Congress might conceivably recruit the "young and ardent part of the community, possessed of but little or no property" to join the militia, while the rest of the men were left defenseless. Such a strategy would deprive the yeomanry of its "boasted weight and strength," and place them at the mercy of their well-armed neighbors. Rather than a band of united patriots fighting for their shared interests, the militia would become a tool of oppression. The Pennsylvania Minority went even further and argued that if Congress could order the militia of one state to put down an insurrection "occasioned by the most galling oppression" in another part of the union, the militiamen may become the "unwilling instruments of tyranny." By coercing the militia into robbing their countrymen of their "liberty and independency," Congress would be forcing these citizens to abandon the defining characteristics of Republican citizenship. The Pennsylvania Minority furthermore feared such an experience would effect an internal, moral change on the militiamen. Not only would the "magnanimity of their minds be extinguished" but "the meaner passions of resentment and revenge" would be increased as well. These passions would then be "the ready and obedient instruments of despotism to enslave others," as previously virtuous citizens are forced into "riveting the chains of despotism on their fellow citizens." Thus, rather than being an expression of their virtue as independent-minded, liberty-loving patriots, service in a militia of this kind would erode that virtue. Reduced to "mere machines" and resembling "Prussian soldiers" more than American citizens, the militiamen would lose their Republican character.

In responding to these arguments against the Constitutional authority given to Congress to raise and support armies and control state militias, The Federalist does not question the fundamental premise of the Anti-Federalist position. The Federalist explicitly states that standing armies are a threat to liberty. In defending the Constitution, The Federalist argues that these military forces are a necessary evil, not a moral good. Rather than question the Anti-Federalists' fear of standing armies, The Federalist leverages this fear in defense of a political structure that will reduce the need for such forces and, to the extent they must exist, prevent them from threatening American liberty. Rather than question the Anti-Federalists' view of standing armies as morally degenerate and incompatible with the American spirit, The Federalist argues that the American people's love of liberty and intolerance of tyranny will play a key role in opposing the excesses of standing armies and militias. The Federalist's treatment of standing armies and nationalized militias is thus subsumed within the larger project of defending energetic government and the system of checks and balances laid out by the Constitutions. The Federalist should not be read as defending standing armies but as defending the wisdom of the governmental system outlined in the Constitution.

The Federalist argued that a single national army and central control over state militias were necessary to defend the nation against foreign foes. John Jay outlines several trade and commercial issues that could bring the United States into conflict with European powers, while Alexander Hamilton argued that hostile Indian tribes threatened America's frontier. Beyond these immediate concerns, the Federalists argued that the "circumstances that endanger the safety of nations are infinite" and impossible to predict. Consequently, the government must not be constrained by "Constitutional shackles" in its attempts to defend the nation from threats as they arise. The Federalist argued that a union and effective government were essential to safeguarding against these threats: "The people of America…consider union and a good national government as necessary to put and keep them in such a situation as instead of inviting war, will tend to repress and discourage it. That situation consists in the best possible state of defense…" In an America lacking union, with each state chiefly responsible for its own defense, foreign powers would find opportunities to exploit the "weakness and divisions" in the country. One state, for example, could be convinced by an invading force to not come to the aid of a neighbor. Even if the states were willing to help one another during an invasion, a lack of national leadership would leave the country unable to respond to the crisis in a coordinated and effective manner. This was precisely the problem under the Articles of Confederation during the War of Independence, when the American war effort was hampered by states that were slow to send their militiamen to fight in other states. Whereas a continuation of such division and disunity would signal weakness and invite foreign incursions, a unified government could "apply the resources and power of the whole to the defence of any particular part" and do so "more easily and expeditiously" than individual state governments acting independently."

Support for a standing army and centrally controlled militia grew out of this faith in union and energetic government. If the national government were to be entrusted with ensuring national security, it must be empowered with the means to accomplish that end. A militia under a single "plan of discipline" and consolidated into a single "corps" would be more efficient than a multitude of "distinct independent forces." However, even a consolidated militia would be insufficient: "The steady operations of war against a regular and disciplined army, can only be successfully conducted by a force of the same kind." Militias simply would not be up to the task of confronting America's enemies: "War, like most other things, is a science to be acquired and perfected by diligence, by perseverance, by time, and by practice." Entrusting the nation's defense to the militia alone would require these citizens to spend an inordinate amount of time training and conducting other duties. This would cost a significant "loss of labor, and disconcertion of the industrious pursuits of individuals." War had become a profession in the modern world, and a standing army was therefore necessary to protect against invasion. The Federalists admitted that, in addition to defending against external threats, the standing army may at times be needed to quell internal sedition and insurrections: "…there might sometimes be a necessity to make use of a force constituted differently from the militia, to preserve the peace of the community, and to maintain the just authority of the laws…" However, the Federalists did not see this as a particularly unusual provision. Just as states relied on their militias to quell uprisings, the national government would need a means of defending its authority.

Despite these arguments for the necessity of national forces, The Federalist should not be read as a defense of standing armies. The Federalists clearly understood the republican concern that excessive dependence on a professional soldiery would degrade the independence and liberty of the citizenry: "The continual necessity for his services enhances the importance of the soldier, and proportionably degrades the condition of the citizens. The military state becomes elevated above the civil. The inhabitants of territories often the theater of war, are unavoidably subjected to frequent infringements on their rights, which serve to weaken their sense of those rights." In time, the citizenry would come to see soldiers not only as "protectors" but as "superiors," thus degrading the people in a passive acquiescence to tyranny. In Federalist #41, James Madison repeatedly referenced the danger that "military establishments" posed to liberty and praised the "prudent jealousy entertained by the people, of standing armies." Large or small, standing armies were the "object of laudable circumspection and precaution." However, despite the risks, the union could not survive without such forces: "A standing force, therefore, is a dangerous, at the same time that it may be a necessary, provision." Hamilton's argument in defense of the Constitution's provisions for national military forces is informed by a similar sense of resigned pragmatism: "…if the defence of the community…should make it necessary to have an army, so numerous as to hazard its liberty, this is one of those calamities for which there is neither preventative nor cure. It cannot be provided against by any possible form of government…" Thus, the question for the Federalists was not whether a national government should be entrusted with military forces. The need for national forces was an unfortunate reality. Instead, The Federalist was concerned with how best to design government such that the risks posed by these forces could be mitigated.

The Federalist argues that the political system outlined in the Constitution would reduce the need for standing armies in the United States. The Federalists feared that without a strong union guided by an energetic government, the several states would be in a continual state of competition and war. "…envy and jealousy would soon extinguish confidence and affection…like most other bordering nations, they would always be either involved in disputes and war, or live in the constant apprehension of them." In Federalist #8, Hamilton paints a bleak picture of life in America following a disintegration of the union. Smaller states would compensate for their inferior natural strength with a well-disciplined standing army. Larger states, having once suffered humiliations at the hands of their smaller neighbors' soldiers, would then quickly establish their own professional militaries. Subject to frequent invasions and the constant threat of war, America, like continental Europe, would come to depend on the soldiery for survival. Rather than view soldiers "with a spirit of jealous acquiescence," the American people would "look up to the military power for protection" and "submit to its oppressions." Since "safety from external danger, is the most powerful director of national conduct," Americans would willingly entrust their liberty to soldiers in exchange for security. Thus, without union, American liberty would ultimately become a casualty of the mutual distrust that inevitably arises between neighbors: "Our liberties would be a prey to the means of defending ourselves against the ambition and jealousy of each other." The risk to liberty posed by standing armies was therefore a powerful argument in favor of union.

The Federalist also used the fear of standing armies to justify the Constitution's provisions for a nationally controlled militia. By empowering the federal government with control over the state militias, the Constitution would diminish the need for a standing army: "If standing armies are dangerous to liberty, an efficacious power over the militia, in the same body [the national government] ought, as far as possible, to take away the inducement and the pretext to such unfriendly institutions." The Federalists sought to force their opponents to choose between the lesser of two evils. The national government needed some means of defending the country and preserving the union. Thus, if the Anti-Federalists were genuine in their opposition to standing armies, then they ought to support a plan that would reduce the need for such forces.

The Federalist further argued that a strong union under an energetic government would remove the need for a "military execution" of the laws so feared by the Anti-Federalists. Under the Articles of Confederation, the national government had no ability to enforce its laws on the citizenry. Although the states were constitutionally bound to obey the laws of the national government, in reality, it was up to the states to decide whether to comply. The result was gridlock and the inability of the United States to implement national policies: "The measures of the union have not been executed; the delinquencies of the states have, step by step, matured themselves to an extreme, which has at length arrested all the wheels of the national government, and brought them to an awful stand." The Federalist saw only two ways out of this situation: the use of military force to implement national legislation or the establishment of an energetic government capable of imposing laws directly on the citizenry without the interference of states. The former solution would be to "substitute the violent and sanguinary agency of the sword, to the mild influence of the magistracy." Enforcing laws "by the coercion of arms" rather than "by the coercion of the magistracy" would furthermore incite civil war among the states and eventually lead to military despotism: "In an association, where the general authority is confined to the collective bodies of the communities that compose it, every breach of the laws must involve a state of war, and military execution must become the only instrument of civil obedience." Instead of accepting such a dangerous state of affairs, The Federalist advocated enabling the federal government to pass laws that would be supreme throughout the land and enforceable on individual citizens. To the objection that the people would not willingly submit to national legislation, The Federalist argued that citizens would in fact be more likely to acquiesce to the national government's laws than to those of state governments. People would be most likely to trust and obey a government based on "the goodness or badness of its administration." The Federalists predicted that, since that the national government would be run by men of greater ability, less subject to the effects of faction and endowed with more comprehensive information regarding the needs of the country, it would ultimately be more effective and respected than state governments. Furthermore, a direct connection between the citizens and the national government would in time "conciliate the respect and attachment of the community." Thus, as opposed to the present confederacy, in which "there can be no sanction for the laws but force," the energetic government proposed by the Constitution sought to base its authority on the affection and support of the citizenry.

The Federalist argues further that, to the extent a standing army must exist, the political system outlined by the Constitution would prevent such a force from threatening American liberty. The Constitution's provisions for delegated authority and separation of powers would prevent the rise of tyranny at the hands of a military force. By entrusting responsibility for raising and supporting armies to the Congress, the Constitution would keep control over the army in the hands of the people: "...it is a full answer to those who require a more peremptory provision against military establishments in time of peace, to say, that the whole power of the proposed government is to be in the hands of the representatives of the people. This is the essential, and, after all, the only efficacious security for the rights and privileges of the people..." By requiring Congress to review appropriations for the army every two years, the Constitution ensured that even a corrupt or careless legislature would not be able to facilitate the rise of a standing army. Since Congress was "not at liberty to invest in the executive department, permanent funds for the support of an army," it would take a considerable amount of time, a sustained conspiracy among all members of Congress and the executive, and multiple election cycles for an army to become so large as to threaten liberty. In the interim, opposition parties could rise against the party in power, win an election and immediately cut off the military's funding. The executive, furthermore, would never be able to acquire a force large enough to coerce Congress into providing funds for the army since there would be no conceivable pretense to obtain such a force in times of peace.

However, the ultimate check on national military forces were the American people themselves. Although, as shown above, The Federalist recognized the risk posed by a standing army to the virtue and independence of the people, it argued that the Constitution would actually enhance the ability of citizens to resist any attempt by a tyrannical government, backed up by professional military forces, to threaten American liberty. Under no circumstances would the people give up their right to the defend their interests against predatory politicians: "If the representatives of the people betray their constituents, there is then no resource left but in the exertion of that original right of self-defence, which is paramount to all positive forms of government…" Popular resistance could be more easily accomplished against national rulers since the states would provide a ready-made form for national resistance. Citizens, The Federalist argued, would actually have more to fear from the usurpation of state authorities since there would be no government around which to rally. However, the federal structure of the American system of government would strengthen the power of the people to resist usurpation from either national or state governments. If the national authorities threatened liberty, the people could resist through the states. If, on the other hand, state authorities abused their powers, the national government would be a means of holding them in check. The people, "by throwing themselves into either scale," would be the ultimate arbiters of the inevitable rivalries between states and the national government. Thus, the people would be "entirely the masters of their own fate," and the guardians of liberty. The natural strength of the community would provide a sure check on the power of standing armies.

The militia would also provide protection against the potential excesses of standing armies and energetic government. Consistent with the republican ideal of a militia indistinguishable from the people, The Federalist dismissed as paranoia the fear that a militia controlled by a national government could somehow be used as an instrument of oppression:

> There is something so far fetched, and so extravagant, in the idea of danger to liberty from the militia…Where, in the name of common sense, are our fears to end, if we may not trust our sons, our brothers, our neighbours, our fellow citizens? What shadow of danger can there be from men, who are daily mingling with the rest of their countrymen; and who participate with them in the same feelings, sentiments, habits, and interests?

Contrary to their opponents' fears of moral corruption in a nationally-controlled militia, The Federalist argued that militiamen would never consent to being the means by which a tyrant deprived the American people of their liberty. Rather than marching to another state to rivet "the chains of slavery upon a part of their countrymen" a militia would more readily crush the tyrants who gave them such unconscionable orders.

In final analysis, The Federalist largely continued the traditional Anglo-American fear of standing armies. Although the defenders of the Constitution thought a union charged with defending the nation must have the ability to command the military power of that nation, the standing army was, at best, a necessary evil and by no means a moral good. Unlike today, when Americans look to their soldiers as paragons of patriotism and civic virtue, the founders viewed professional warriors as the antithesis of republican citizenship. Subservient, avaricious, crude, and unprincipled, soldiers were symbols of the moral decay and unchecked tyranny America had fought a war to escape. The Americans of the late 18th century imagined themselves as the pioneers of a new political system, a community founded on virtue, governed by choice, and held together by a sense of duty to one's countrymen. Standing armies and militias under the distant control of a national government had no place in such a system. After all, American freedom had been won by ordinary citizens unwilling to submit to a corrupt monarch, not by professional soldiers whose character and interests were defined by war. Rather than challenge this view of America's founding, the Federalists used it to defend the proposed Constitution. A strong union and energetic government with control over state militias would reduce the need for standing armies and a military execution of the laws. To the extent that professional military forces must exist, the system of delegated authority and checks and balances outlined by the Constitution would ensure that the representatives of the people kept the soldiery under their control. If the checks and balances at the national level somehow failed, the people would still have recourse to their states and militias to counter the ambition of tyrants. Despite the protestations of the Constitution's opponents, the Federalists' position implied a fundamental faith in the strength of the American spirit. It was inconceivable to the Federalists that a standing army could ever become so powerful as to threaten the American people's jealously guarded liberty, and the notion that a nationally controlled militia might somehow lose the character of citizens and turn on their countrymen was dismissed as absurd. Thus, in providing for national military forces, the Constitution did not propose an abandonment of the principles that won American independence. Rather, it was an enduring faith in the strength of those principles that made standing armies a tolerable risk.

Author of ClassicNote and Sources

Brittany Nelson and Christopher Higgins (second revision 09/15/2011), author of ClassicNote. Completed on September 10, 2000, copyright held by GradeSaver.

Updated and revised Elizabeth Weinbloom December 30, 2011. Copyright held by GradeSaver.

Amar, Akhil Reed.. America's Constitution: A Biography. New York: Random House, 2005.

Ralph Ketcham. The Anti-Federalist Papers and the Constitutional Convention Debates. New York: New American Library, 1986.

Cecelia M. Kenyon. The Antifederalists. Indianapolis: Bobbs-Merrill, 1966.

George W. Carey and James McClellan. The Federalist. Indianapolis: Liberty Fund, 2001.

Storing, Herbert J. What the Anti-Federalists Were For. Chicago: University of Chicago Press, 1981.

Richard H. Kohn. Anglo-American Antimilitary Tracts. New York: Arno Press, 1979.

Clinton Rossiter,. Hamilton and the Constitution. NYC: Harcourt, Brace, & World, Inc, 1964.

The Impartial Examiner. ""Anti-Federalist Papers: The Impartial Examiner.".." 2011-08-04. <http://www.constitution.org/afp/impar_exam.htm.>.

Hamilton, Alexander, John Jay, James Madison. The Federalist Papers.

Essay: A Close Reading of James Madison's The Federalist No. 51 and its Relevancy Within the Sphere of Modern Political Thought

by Anonymous
March 05, 2005

The roots of republican government and democratic ideals are firmly planted in James Madison's "The Federalist No. 51, The Structure of the Government Must Furnish the Proper Checks and Balances Between the Different Departments." Written on February 6, 1788, this essay is one of three documents that make up a group of political pieces known as The Federalist Papers. These documents were written by the three main proponents of the U.S. Constitution and the Federal Convention; Alexander Hamilton, John Jay, and James Madison (Mulford 999). The collection of essays was first published in the Independent Journal, a political magazine based in New York, in addition to several other magazines. Ironically, the governor of New York, George Clinton, was an Anti-Federalist, an antagonist of governmental liberties, republican ideals, and the subsequent ratification of the U.S. Constitution (Mulford 999). "The Federalist No. 51" was written a year after Hamilton concluded that the state of New York would not ratify the Constitution. Subsequently, The Federalist Papers were published and widely disseminated in New York, in addition to several other states, in order to persuade and convince the Anti-Federalists to support the foundations of democratic republicanism and federalism.

Historical Background: In a sweeping attempt to rejuvenate the national government and replace its nebulous Articles of Confederation with a more stable legal and governing document, the Federalists assembled in what came to be known as the Federal Convention. This covert meeting was held from the spring through the fall of 1787, and was the genesis of the United States Constitution (Mulford 998). Before its nationwide ratification, the Anti-Federalists, who claimed that the document did not represent the lower and middle classes in society, staunchly opposed the Federalist's version of the Constitution. They were later appeased by the proposal and subsequent implementation of the Bill of Rights in 1789 and 1790 when the First Congress of the United States presented the first twelve amendments to the state legislatures for ratification (NARA). The federal Constitution was finally ratified by all thirteen states in 1790 (Mulford 999). The Constitution is a living document that has the embedded capacity to be amended by the legislative branch of government by means of a three-fourths approval vote by the state legislatures. It has been amended twenty-seven times, with the final amendment disallowing U.S. Senators to set or increase their own salaries (U.S. Constitution). The Constitution remains to be one of the most unique governing documents in the world because of its assemblage of personal freedoms and checks and balances between the executive, legislative, and judiciary institutions of our government.

Document Summary: An advocate of individual liberties and democratic structures and processes in government, James Madison purports his ideas of a governmental system buttressed with a division of powers and independent institutions in "The Federalist No. 51." Madison asserts that the legislative branch is the most powerful branch of government and in the most need of checks and balances from the other branches, in order to ensure that no one branch becomes tyrannical. Furthermore, Madison claims the importance of guarding our country from not only the tyrannical rule of an executive leader, but also from the injustices that may ensue from groups of private citizens. Finally, Madison supports the idea that justice should be the overall purpose of representative government and a strong force among citizens in a civil society.

Analysis:

"The Federalist No. 51" is relevant to the canon of modern political thought because it encapsulates the founding principles of federalism, protection against tyranny, the inevitability of class conflict, and the principled solution of checks and balances. Madison, unlike Hamilton and other political activists of his time, supported the preservation of state governments, a pluralistic theory whose essence necessitates the existence of state government for the solidification of liberty and national cohesiveness among the states. Madison utilizes strong and persuasive rhetoric throughout his argument. He specifically states who is audience is in the salutation of his argument, "To the People of the State of New York" (Madison 1). Madison's purpose in "The Federalist No. 51" is twofold: First, to persuade the Anti-Federalist citizens and government of New York, a key state in the ratification of the Constitution, to support the Federalist's ideals; second, to inform the Federalist citizens of New York about the full message of the Federalist Party. Therefore, Madison can be credited with many of the founding principles that are necessary for our current Republic to exist.

One of the first channels that Madison uses to define our modern understanding of political thought is an emphasis on federalism. He claims that the only way freedom and liberty can be maintained is through the institution of federalism, "in order to lay a due foundation for that separate and distinct exercise of the different powers of government/is admitted on all hands to be essential to the preservation of liberty, it is evident that each department should have a will of its own" (Madison 1). Madison supports the idea of separated governmental entities by acknowledging the existence of their individual wills. Without this acknowledgement, the institutions of government would not be powerful enough to function independently. Madison points out the danger of any one institution harboring too much power "It is important in a republic not only to guard the society against the oppression of its rulers, but to guard one part of the society against the injustice of the other part" (3). Madison further asserts that since the people of America transferred their sovereignty to the government, then in turn, "a double security arises to the rights of the people" (3). This claim is relevant to the foundation of modern political thought because it places a value on the citizens of the states and ensures them protection from a sovereign in exchange for their sovereignty.

Madison embraces one of the primary arguments of the Anti-Federalist movement, recognition of the lower and middle classes in society. Madison recognizes the existence of class distinction and the tyranny the majority often has over the minority. He further recognizes this distinction within the same department of government. Madison proposes a legal solution to this apparent problem, "giving to those who administer each department the necessary constitutional means and personal motives to resist encroachments of the others" (Madison 2). His 'eye for an eye' solution and discussion of human nature may stem from Thomas Hobbes's philosophical insights into the state of nature and civil society. In addition, Madison employs Biblical allusion throughout this discourse on political inequality, "if men were angels, no government would be necessary" (2). Here, Madison recognizes man's state of imperfection and need for government control. Furthermore, Madison claims that a power "independent of the people" would be a mandatory existence because of the inherent factionalism among the classes of citizens in America. Madison shows his unbiased nature by proposing that the Federalist concepts are a necessary existence because of human nature and class factionalism, a force that exists outside of Madison's own persuasive rhetoric.

Personal Reflection: I am a strong advocate of federalism and like Madison; I support an inherent system of checks and balances in order to prevent tyranny from either the majority or minority groups in a given society. I speculate, however, if Madison could have predicted the permanent ability of one branch to declare acts of another branch unconstitutional, i.e. Marbury v. Madison (1803) 5 U.S. 137. Madison firmly claims that the legislative branch of the federal system is the most powerful branch of government (Madison 1). A legislative veto overrides the effects of an executive veto, however, the judicial branch and should never be ignored. United States Supreme Court appointments are the longest lasting legacy of any U.S. President who has the opportunity to appoint a new justice to the bench. The Supreme Court does not make new law; however, it has and will continue to declare acts of the legislature unconstitutional. However, the legislative branch remains to be the most powerful branch because of its recourse over the executive branch. Madison was correct in recommending a system of checks and balances as a solution to tyranny and political hegemony. His solution is important to the overall canon of political thought because it holds political leaders and their individual institutions accountable to the populace. This separates the democratic system from monarchies or autocracies that cannot ensure the same fundamental freedoms and protections to its citizenry.

Conclusion: By closely examining the origins behind and meanings within Madison's work, readers can fully appreciate the overall impact it has on the canon of modern political theory. "The Federalist No. 51" can be credited with the foundations of republican government and the institutions of federalism, protection against tyranny, and fundamental solution of checks and balances. Madison's paper can be seen as the foundation of the U.S. Constitution and the premise of individual rights and freedoms. Madison's work differs from the other essays in The Federalist Papers because Madison, unlike Hamilton and Jay, recognized the importance of the existence and relationship between state governments and the national government. This is important today because of issues in state and individual sovereignty, as well as funding and resource preservation. "The Federalist No. 51" is the foundation of our forefathers' creation of a great republic, with embedded protections against an oppressor, and the capacity to protect and maintain individual freedoms.

Works Cited

Madison, James. "The Federalist No. 51: The Structure of the Government Must Furnish the Proper Checks and Balances Between the Different Departments." The Constitution Society. Texas, 1995. (Madison). Internet Available: http://www.http://ecu.blackboard.com/bin/common/course.pl?course_id=_20911_1&frame:

Mulford, Carla, Angela Vietto, and Amy E. Winans, eds. Early American Writings. New York: Oxford UP, 2002. (Mulford).

"The Constitution of the United States," Amend. XXVI, sect.1&3. (U.S. Constitution).

Essay: Lock, Hobbes, and the Federalist Papers

by Anonymous
January 30, 2006

The Federalist Papers, written by Jay, Madison, and Hamilton, were laid out in order to convince the individual states to ratify the new U.S. Constitution and defend a central government. Many times the words of these Founding Fathers echoed those of 17th century authors Thomas Hobbes and John Locke. Federalist #10, #51, and #78, all bear resemblance to either or both of these philosophers, especially Locke's *Two Treatises of Government* and Hobbes' *Leviathan*. Many of the essays found in the Federalist Papers are in one way or another based on these two gentlemen, and specifically these two works.

In Federalist #10, James Madison addresses the problem of factions, and the problematic inability to dissolve these factions. He writes that factions are impossible to dissolve without taking away liberty, thus the best course of action is to take power away from the factions and attempt to control them. This is very similar to Hobbes' view of the "state of nature". According to Madison, a society with unchecked factions is likely to run rampant and wild, such as that described in *Leviathan*. Madison argues that factions exist to join people with similar passions or ideas and allows them to fight against what they consider wrong. Naturally, this causes animosity and warring between groups, because, according to Hobbes, "If any two men desire the same thing, which nevertheless they cannot both enjoy, they become enemies; and in their way to the End, endeavor to destroy, or subdue one an other." However, the liberty that allows these factions to exist cannot be taken away. Locke grants all the "natural rights" of "life, health, liberty, and possessions", something which Madison agrees with and defends.

The question arises of how to control these factions while still allowing them to have these "natural rights". Madison's answer, which resembles Locke, is to have a representative government. A government who gets its power from those it leads. Madison also argues that this government must be made up of a large number of people, so that it is "less probable that a majority of the whole will have a common motive to invade the rights of other citizens." Ideally, this representation of people will be prohibitive to Hobbes' constant state of war and violence. Both Madison's Federalist #10 and Locke's Two Treatises of Government agree that in the natural state, factions or groups will emerge against one another, and the best way to control these groups is through a representative governing body, made up of enough people to remain impartial, so that any one faction cannot rise up and gain authoritarian power.

Federalist #51 discusses the need for power to be separated amongst various branches of the government, so that one single group cannot rise up and gain total control. Madison states that by "so contriving the interior structure of the government as that its several constituent parts may, by their mutual relations, be the means of keeping each other in their proper places." Similarly, as Locke suggests, the government will only have the powers that the people give it. Should the government overstep its bounds and infringe on the natural rights of man, Locke gives the people the right to revolt, because the government has breached a social contract. By spreading the power out and only allowing the government to control that which it is given by the people, the possibility that one group will rise up is eliminated.

Federalist #78, written by Alexander Hamilton, discusses the role of the judiciary and the need for a judiciary separated from the executive and legislative branches. Locke supports the development of a judicial branch. In his words, "Those who are united into one body, and have a common established law and judicature to appeal to, with authority to decide controversies between them, and punish offenders, are in civil society one with another: but those who have no such common appeal, I mean on earth, are still in the state of nature, each being, where there is no other, judge for himself, and executioner; which is, as I have before shewed it, the perfect state of nature." Forming a judicial branch furthers the development of a "civil society" and takes people away from the "state of nature". Hamilton also views the judicial branch as relatively harmless. He states the judicial branch is the least powerful because it cannot "attack with success either of the other two." Hamilton proposes that the judicial branch will be the foundation of a limited Constitution. The courts can determine legislation as well as the acts of the executive branch to be unconstitutional, and therefore check the other two branches. This proposition would fall in line with Locke's philosophy of keeping power spread thin in order to limit the influence of factions. Hobbes on the other hand would be less likely to support having a separate judicial branch. Hobbes declares "He therefore that is partial in judgement, doth what in him lies to deter men from the use of judges and arbitrators, and consequently, against the fundamental law of nature, is the cause of war." Since the nature of man is greedy, selfish, and cruel, having an impartial judge becomes nearly nonexistent. However, this argument is defeated by Locke, whose separated powers prevents partial judgment.

Throughout each of these three essays from *The Federalist Papers*, Hobbes and Locke's influence is seen time and again. Hamilton, Jay, and Madison, took the different views of the state of nature and found ways to improve Hobbes' "poor, nasty, brutish, and short" life, by incorporating some of Locke's ideas to eliminate the state of nature. By limiting factions, spreading out power, and creating a separate judicial system, the Founding Fathers created a government that gains its power from those it governs and a government, as Locke says, that can govern itself first.

Quiz 1

1. **Who is the author of The Federalist Papers?**
   A. James Madison
   B. John Jay
   C. Alexander Hamilton
   D. All of the above

2. **Under which anonymous name were the Federalist Papers published?**
   A. Sunius
   B. Constitution
   C. Publius
   D. None of the above

3. **Who wrote the majority of the Federalist Papers?**
   A. James Madison
   B. John Jay
   C. Alexander Hamilton
   D. None of the above

4. **How many papers did John Jay write?**
   A. Six
   B. Two
   C. Five
   D. Four

5. **About which subject does John Jay primarily write about?**
   A. Foreign Affairs
   B. Factions
   C. The Bill of Rights
   D. Internal Affairs

6. **What subject is Federalist #10 primarily about?**
   A. Factions
   B. Foreign affairs
   C. The Bill of Rights
   D. Internal Affairs

7. **Who wrote Federalist #10?**
   A. James Madison
   B. John Jay
   C. Alexander Hamilton
   D. None of the above

8. **What was Alexander Hamilton's opinion on the Bill of Rights, as expressed in The Federalist Papers?**
   A. He was for the Constitution including it before ratification
   B. He thought that the Bill of Rights were primarily unnecessary
   C. He was for the Bill of Rights being included as amendments
   D. None of the above

9. **What did Hamilton believe was the source of power in the republican form of government?**
   A. Factions
   B. The people
   C. The Constitution
   D. The knowledge of the elite

10. **In the last Federalist Paper, #85, what philosopher does Hamilton quote?**
    A. Hume
    B. Locke
    C. Plato
    D. Montesquieu

11. **According to James Madison, what is the doctrine of separation of powers?**
    A. Both of the above
    B. Three generally separate branch of government with some interaction
    C. A complete and separate operations of the three branches of government
    D. None of the above

12. **What characteristics does Hamilton believe is most important in the executive branch?**
    A. Energy
    B. Equity
    C. Fairness
    D. None of the above

13. **What does the Federalist Papers believe of the people who drafted the constitution?**
    A. They were remarkable men, perfect in all that they do
    B. They were men who had nothing else to do
    C. They were remarkable men, but still not perfect
    D. None of the above

14. **What does John Jay believe are two guaranteed facts of political life?**
    A. Some form of government is necessary in a society and all forms of government must be granted sufficient power to regulate conflict and administer the laws
    B. Some form of government is necessary in a society and government must earn the right to be granted sufficient power to regulate conflict and administer laws
    C. Some form of government is necessary in a society and all politicians are only out for their best interest
    D. Some form of government is not necessary but useful in a society and all forms of government must be granted sufficient power to regulate conflict and administer laws

15. **In what way did the authors of the Federalist paper believe the country was united?**
    A. Manners and customs
    B. Language
    C. Geography
    D. All of above

16. **Why is the government safer from foreign threats under the new Constitution, according to the Federalist Papers?**
    A. Neither a nor b
    B. A national government will have more men of intellect in order to carry out the laws
    C. both The country will not have to make thirteen different treaties and foreign governments will only have to deal with one national government and A national government will have more men of intellect in order to carry out the laws
    D. The country will not have to make thirteen different treaties and foreign governments will only have to deal with one national government

17. **What does Hamilton believe will be the end result of the Articles of Confederation?**
    A. Anarchy
    B. A government that consistently protects liberty
    C. A government that is adequate, but does not always protect liberty
    D. None of the above

According to the Federalist Papers, what is the role of a standing army in the country?

A. A standing army protects liberty and is necessary for the functioning of the government

B. A standing army is at odds with liberty

C. A standing army is not necessary

D. None of the above

19. For Hamilton, what is the principal purpose of the Union?
  A. The preservation of public peace, the regulation of commerce
  B. The conducting of foreign affairs.
  C. Common defense of the members
  D. All of the above

20. In what state were the Papers published?
  A. New York
  B. Massachusetts
  C. Virginia
  D. Rhode Island

21. In what form were the papers published?
  A. Newspaper, all at once
  B. Magazine
  C. Newspaper, one at a time over a series of weeks
  D. A book

22. To what end were the Federalist Papers published?
  A. In order to convince the delegates to attend the Constitutional Convention
  B. In order to support the Articles of Confederation
  C. In order to convince the politicians of New York to support the Constitution
  D. In order to convince the people of New York to ratify the convention

23. What two important principles does Madison cite were in conflict in #37?
  A. Stability and energy
  B. Stability and liberty
  C. Energy and liberty
  D. Liberty and justice

24. Which philosopher executed the most influence during the Revolutionary Era?
  A. Hume
  B. Montesqieu
  C. Locke
  D. None of the above

25. Hamilton was from which state?

    A. New York

    B. Massachusetts

    C. Virginia

    D. Rhode Island

Quiz 1 Answer Key

1. **(D)** All of the above
2. **(C)** Publius
3. **(C)** Alexander Hamilton
4. **(A)** Six
5. **(A)** Foreign Affairs
6. **(A)** Factions
7. **(A)** James Madison
8. **(B)** He thought that the Bill of Rights were primarily unnecessary
9. **(B)** The people
10. **(A)** Hume
11. **(B)** Three generally separate branch of government with some interaction
12. **(A)** Energy
13. **(C)** They were remarkable men, but still not perfect
14. **(A)** Some form of government is necessary in a society and all forms of government must be granted sufficient power to regulate conflict and administer the laws
15. **(D)** All of above
16. **(C)** both The country will not have to make thirteen different treaties and foreign governments will only have to deal with one national government and A national government will have more men of intellect in order to carry out the laws
17. **(A)** Anarchy
18. **(A)** A standing army protects liberty and is necessary for the functioning of the government
19. **(D)** All of the above
20. **(A)** New York
21. **(C)** Newspaper, one at a time over a series of weeks
22. **(D)** In order to convince the people of New York to ratify the convention
23. **(B)** Stability and liberty
24. **(C)** Locke
25. **(A)** New York

Quiz 2

1. **James Madison was from which state?**
    A. New York
    B. Massachusetts
    C. Virginia
    D. Rhode Island

2. **What function did John Jay serve under the Articles of Confederation?**
    A. Vice President
    B. Secretary of Foreign affairs
    C. President
    D. Ambassador

3. **According to Madison, what is the main threat to government?**
    A. People
    B. Foreign governments
    C. Factions
    D. None of the above

4. **The Senate mirrors what Britain body?**
    A. House of Lords
    B. House of Commons
    C. All of the above

5. **According to Hamilton, what was one of the main criticisms of the executive branch**
    A. President may be re-elected
    B. President has too much power
    C. Presidential term is too long
    D. Presidential term is not long enough

6. **Which government does the founding fathers believe is the most ideal?**
    A. Sparta
    B. Britain
    C. Rome
    D. None of the above

7. **According to Madison, where does self-government flourish?**
    A. A small, homogenous land
    B. A large diverse land
    C. All of the above

8. **According to Madison, what is the general purpose of government?**
    A. Justice
    B. Commerce
    C. Peace
    D. None of the above

9. **What are the differences between the qualification requirements of representatives and senators?**
    A. Neither a nor b
    B. both Senators have to be older and Senators have to be citizens of the United States longer
    C. Senators have to be citizens of the United States longer
    D. Senators have to be older

10. **What do foreign governments look for in a Senate?**
    A. Neither a nor b
    B. A government that is constantly in turmoil
    C. both A stable government that is able to conduct foreign affairs and A government that is constantly in turmoil
    D. A stable government that is able to conduct foreign affairs

11. **What depends on the vitality of the Presidency, according to Alexander Hamilton?**
    A. National defense
    B. Protection of property rights
    C. Sound administration of the law
    D. All of the above

12. **How many papers are in the Federalist Papers?**
    A. 75
    B. 80
    C. 85
    D. 90

13. **According to Alexander Hamilton, what characteristic must an energetic Executive branch have?**
    A. Certain degree of secrecy
    B. Sufficient powers
    C. Unity
    D. All of the above

14. **Which branch, according to Alexander Hamilton, is the weakest?**
    A. Judicial
    B. Executive
    C. Legislative
    D. None of the above

15. **Under the Constitution, how long are judges appointed?**
    A. For life, given good behavior
    B. For life, no exceptions
    C. Until age 65
    D. Until age 75

16. **What is the primary advantage of a strong union under a signle national government Jay cites in paper #4?**
    A. A strong union will lead to future cultural accomplishments
    B. A strong union will better protect against foreign aggression
    C. A strong union will disuade states from rebelling
    D. A strong union will be better able to quell internal dissent

17. **In paper #5, Jay uses historical examples from which country to argue in support of uniting America under a single national government?**
    A. Great Britain
    B. Germany
    C. Greece
    D. France

18. **in paper 7, what does Hamilton warn might happen if America adopts a system of multiple, independent sovereignties instead of a union?**
    A. War between the states and interference from foreign powers
    B. A weak education system
    C. Limited artistic achievements
    D. Economic collapse

19. **What kind of military force does Hamilton discuss in paper #11?**
    A. Militia
    B. Cavalry
    C. Army
    D. Navy

20. **In paper 12, Hamilton argues that a strong union will lead to a more effective**
    A. Military
    B. Tax system
    C. Diplomatic corps
    D. University system

21. **In paper 13, Hamilton aruges that, compared to a system of independent states or confederacies, a union would be**
    A. Larger
    B. More encumbered by large redundant bureacracies
    C. More cost effective
    D. Less cost effective

22. **In paper 14, Madison discusses the relationship between**
    A. The media and the presidency
    B. System of government and size of a country
    C. The system of government and religion
    D. Taxes and politics

23. **In paper 17, Hamilton discusses the relationship between**
    A. The President and the Senate
    B. National government and the States
    C. Banks and politicians
    D. The Supreme Court and the House of Representatives

24. **Paper 18 references the history of what country?**
    A. Great Britain
    B. Rome
    C. Greece
    D. France

25. **Paper 19 cites the history of what country?**
     A. Britain
     B. Germany
     C. Rome
     D. Greece

Quiz 2 Answer Key

1. **(C)** Virginia
2. **(B)** Secretary of Foreign affairs
3. **(C)** Factions
4. **(A)** House of Lords
5. **(A)** President may be re-elected
6. **(B)** Britain
7. **(B)** A large diverse land
8. **(A)** Justice
9. **(B)** both Senators have to be older and Senators have to be citizens of the United States longer
10. **(C)** both A stable government that is able to conduct foreign affairs and A government that is constantly in turmoil
11. **(D)** All of the above
12. **(C)** 85
13. **(D)** All of the above
14. **(A)** Judicial
15. **(A)** For life, given good behavior
16. **(B)** A strong union will better protect against foreign aggression
17. **(A)** Great Britain
18. **(A)** War between the states and interference from foreign powers
19. **(D)** Navy
20. **(B)** Tax system
21. **(C)** More cost effective
22. **(B)** System of government and size of a country
23. **(B)** National government and the States
24. **(C)** Greece
25. **(B)** Germany

Quiz 3

1. **Paper 20 cites the history of what country?**
   A. Great Britain
   B. Germany
   C. The Netherlands
   D. France

2. **Paper 21 criticizes what system of government?**
   A. Monarchy
   B. Democracy
   C. Confederacy
   D. Constitutional Monarchy

3. **Paper 24 deals with concerns about the existence of standing armies under what conditions?**
   A. Times of peace
   B. Wartime
   C. Civil war
   D. Arms races with foreign powers

4. **In paper 25, Hamilton argues that people are likely to be most suspicious of what kind of government?**
   A. National government
   B. City government
   C. Town government
   D. State government

5. **In paper 26, what constitutional provision does Hamilton argue will help protect against the emergence of military rule?**
   A. Congressional appropriations of funds for the military every two years
   B. Strong militias
   C. The supreme court
   D. Presidential veto power

6. **In Paper 27, Hamilton argues that people's support for a particular government depends on**
   A. The religion of the president
   B. The prevailing tax rate
   C. The racial composition of the congress
   D. The goodness or badness of its administration

7. **In paper 28, what does Hamilton argue will serve as a natural check on the national government?**
    A. Foreign powers
    B. The media
    C. The Supreme Court
    D. State government

8. **In paper 29, Hamilton defends federal powers over what?**
    A. The coast guard
    B. State militias
    C. State government
    D. Local courts

9. **Which of the following was a major weakness of the Articles of Confederation according to the Federalist papers?**
    A. The inability of the national government to impose taxes directly on the people
    B. Too much executive authority
    C. Religious intolerance
    D. Insufficient respect for state rights

10. **Which of the following was feared by prominent anti-federalists?**
    A. Equal voting rights for women
    B. The extensive taxation powers of the national government leading to tyranny
    C. A weak central government
    D. A weak standing army

11. **Which of the following do state and federal governments share?**
    A. The power to govern interstate commerce
    B. The power to declare war
    C. Exclusive powers
    D. Concurrent powers

12. **The "necessary and proper" clause comes from which Article of the Constitution?**
    A. Article I
    B. Article V
    C. Article II
    D. Article III

13. **In paper 34, Hamilton argues that the national government's power to tax must not be limited since**
    A. Bureacracies tend to expand
    B. The coming war with Britain would require lots of money
    C. It might slow economic growth
    D. It is impossible to know what future crisis and challenges will require

14. **Hamilton argues that it is unnecessary to create a constitutional provision guaranteeing that the House of Representatives had members from all classes of people since**
    A. Certain classes can still represent those from other classes
    B. The wealthy make for the best leaders
    C. It was just impractical
    D. Proportional representation might lead to mob rule

15. **Which of the following did Hamilton argue would aid in tax collection by the national government?**
    A. The Army
    B. The states' tax-collecting apparatus
    C. Merchants
    D. The IRS

16. **According to Madison, the federal government should have the power to**
    A. Limit criticisms of the president
    B. Guarantee the republican form of government in each state
    C. Ban states from having militias
    D. Outlaw certain religions

17. **In paper 45, Madison argues that, historically, local governments**
    A. Were far weaker than national governments
    B. Were not trusted by the people
    C. Prevailed over national governments
    D. Did not exist

18. **According to Madison in paper 46, what do the federal and state governments have in common?**
    A. Both are accountable to the people
    B. Both share the power to declare war
    C. Both can regulate interstate commerce
    D. Both are accountable to God

19. **Which of the following is NOT an argument Madison uses to defend the provision for biennial elections of Congressmen?**
    A. Congressmen need sufficient time to understand the complex issues at the federal level
    B. One year would not be enough time to remove corrupt politicians from office
    C. Voters might lose interest in voting if elections were held too often
    D. Congress cannot change the fundamental form of government

20. **The Constitution apportions representatives for each state according to what?**
    A. Property value
    B. GDP
    C. Territorial size
    D. Population

21. **According to Madison, "nothing less than the chains of despotism can restrain them from destroying and devouring on another" unless the people possess what?**
    A. Wealth
    B. Virtue
    C. Knowledge of current affairs
    D. Faith in God

22. **In paper 56, Madison argues that as the country develops the interests of the various States**
    A. will become similar
    B. will lead to unsolvable problems
    C. will require another revolution
    D. will differ drastically

23. **Who determines the time, place, and manner of elections to the House of Representatives?**
    A. The governors of each state
    B. The Supreme Court
    C. The national government
    D. State courts

24. **According to Hamilton, which of the following is one of the advantages of reelecting the entire House of Represenatives every two years?**
    A. It ensures that polticians' salaries don't get too high
    B. It helps ensure that the same detrimental "spirit" or "faction" will not continue long in Congress
    C. It ensures young people stay active in politics
    D. It ensures that fresh ideas are brought in regularly

25. **The support of what percentage of the House of Representatives is needed to ratify a treaty?**
    A. 50%
    B. 75%
    C. 0%. The House does not ratify treaties.
    D. Two-thirds

Quiz 3 Answer Key

1. **(C)** The Netherlands
2. **(C)** Confederacy
3. **(A)** Times of peace
4. **(A)** National government
5. **(A)** Congressional appropriations of funds for the military every two years
6. **(D)** The goodness or badness of its administration
7. **(D)** State government
8. **(B)** State militias
9. **(A)** The inability of the national government to impose taxes directly on the people
10. **(B)** The extensive taxation powers of the national government leading to tyranny
11. **(D)** Concurrent powers
12. **(A)** Article I
13. **(D)** It is impossible to know what future crisis and challenges will require
14. **(A)** Certain classes can still represent those from other classes
15. **(B)** The states' tax-collecting apparatus
16. **(B)** Guarantee the republican form of government in each state
17. **(C)** Prevailed over national governments
18. **(A)** Both are accountable to the people
19. **(C)** Voters might lose interest in voting if elections were held too often
20. **(D)** Population
21. **(B)** Virtue
22. **(A)** will become similar
23. **(C)** The national government
24. **(B)** It helps ensure that the same detrimental "spirit" or "faction" will not continue long in Congress
25. **(C)** 0%. The House does not ratify treaties.

Quiz 4

1. **Which of the following is not a power of the Senate?**
   - A. Vote on legislation
   - B. Impeach the Presisdent
   - C. Ratify treaties
   - D. Serve as a court for the trial of impeachment

2. **According to the Federalist Paers, what was the intent behind creating the electoral college?**
   - A. Increase the power of the common man
   - B. Make the process as democratic as possible
   - C. Avoid instability
   - D. Ensure elections are controlled by the most educated members of society

3. **The Anti-Federalists feared that the president would come to be**
   - A. A monarch
   - B. A mob boss
   - C. A powerless puppet of Congress
   - D. A celebrity

4. **How many terms should the President be limited to according to the Federalist Papers?**
   - A. 1
   - B. 2
   - C. 4
   - D. There were no term limits on the Presidency in the original Constitution

5. **Hamilton argues that a presidential veto is necessary in order to do what?**
   - A. To ensure that the Courts were not too powerful
   - B. To keep the bureacracy in check
   - C. Hold legislative power in check
   - D. Ensure that the President had the most power in government

6. **According to Hamilton, a veto is which of the following?**
   - A. Not very important in the long run
   - B. An absolute negative
   - C. An essential source of power for the Supreme Court
   - D. A qualified negative since Congress can still overrule it

7. **According to the Supreme Court, who can overrule a Presidential pardon?**
   A. The Speaker of the House
   B. The Chief Justice of the Supreme Court
   C. No one
   D. A majority of state legislatures

8. **Who is the Commander in Chief?**
   A. The President
   B. The Speaker of the House
   C. The Secretary of Defense
   D. The Chairman of the Joint Chiefs of Staff

9. **Who appoints public officials?**
   A. The President, with the advice and consent of the Senate
   B. The Senate, subject to the approval of the Supreme Court
   C. The House of Representatives, subject to the approval of the President
   D. The Supreme Court

10. **In Paper 77, who does Hamilton think would have the most influence?**
    A. The President
    B. A Senator
    C. A Supreme Court Justice
    D. The Speaker of the House of Representatives

11. **Over which of the following types of cases should the Federal judiciary not have authority according to Hamilton?**
    A. Cases that relate to federal law
    B. Violations of state laws
    C. Maritime disputes
    D. Cases that relate to the US Constitution

12. **Who has the power to establish inferior courts?**
    A. The President
    B. The Senate, subject to the approval of the Supreme Court
    C. Congress
    D. The Chief Justice of the Supreme Court

13. **Hamilton argues that State and Federal courts**
   A. could never have deal with similar issues
   B. dealt with the exact same cases
   C. should be thought of as being part of "one whole"
   D. had no relationship whatsoever

14. **Which of the following is NOT explicity guaranteed by the original constitution defended by the Federalist Papers?**
   A. The power of the President to appoint officials
   B. Right to trial by jury in civil cases
   C. The right of citizens to vote for Congressmen
   D. The power of Congress to pass laws

15. **The Federalist Papers were written primarily to convice voters of which state to support the Constitution?**
   A. Pennsylvania
   B. Georgia
   C. New York
   D. Virginia

16. **Which of the following did not concern the Anti-Federalists?**
   A. Standing Armies
   B. Monarchy
   C. The power of the national government
   D. Their own state militias

17. **By "energy," the Federalist means the ability of the government to**
   A. address national problems
   B. expand the country's borders
   C. hold frequent sessions of Congress
   D. legislate swiftly

18. **Delegated authority means**
   A. unelected officials using their power to appoint representatives
   B. elected officials using their power to appoint representatives
   C. unappointed citizens making decisions on behalf of others
   D. elected representatives given the power to make decisions

19. **The essential element of republican government is**
    A. a legislature
    B. a judiciary
    C. a free press
    D. an executive

20. **The anti-Federalists supported**
    A. a weak central government and weak state governments
    B. a weak central government and strong state governments
    C. a strong central government and weak state governments
    D. a strong central government and strong state governments

21. **The Federalists supported**
    A. a weak central government and weak state governments
    B. a strong central government and weak state governments
    C. a weak central government and strong state governments
    D. a strong central government and strong state governments

22. **The creation of the office of the presidency was influenced by**
    A. the legislature of post-revolutionary France
    B. the monarchs of Britain
    C. the emperors of the Roman empire
    D. the consuls of the Roman republic

23. **The English Bill of Rights established**
    A. the priimacy of the monarch
    B. the freedom of speech
    C. the freedom of religion
    D. the primacy of the legislature

24. **The factions feared by the Federalist Papers can be found in modern politics in**
    A. lobby groups
    B. third parties
    C. the media
    D. watchdog organizations

25. **The Federalist Papers claim that the Constitution was designed to prevent leaders like**
    A. Napoleon
    B. Oliver Cromwell
    C. Alexander the Great
    D. King Ludwig II

Quiz 4 Answer Key

1. **(B)** Impeach the Presisdent
2. **(C)** Avoid instability
3. **(A)** A monarch
4. **(D)** There were no term limits on the Presidency in the original Constitution
5. **(C)** Hold legislative power in check
6. **(D)** A qualified negative since Congress can still overrule it
7. **(C)** No one
8. **(A)** The President
9. **(A)** The President, with the advice and consent of the Senate
10. **(A)** The President
11. **(B)** Violations of state laws
12. **(C)** Congress
13. **(C)** should be thought of as being part of "one whole"
14. **(B)** Right to trial by jury in civil cases
15. **(C)** New York
16. **(D)** Their own state militias
17. **(A)** address national problems
18. **(D)** elected representatives given the power to make decisions
19. **(A)** a legislature
20. **(B)** a weak central government and strong state governments
21. **(B)** a strong central government and weak state governments
22. **(D)** the consuls of the Roman republic
23. **(D)** the primacy of the legislature
24. **(A)** lobby groups
25. **(B)** Oliver Cromwell

ClassicNotes

GradeSaver™

Getting you the grade since 1999™

Other ClassicNotes from GradeSaver™

1984
A&P and Other Stories
Absalom, Absalom
Adam Bede
The Adventures of Augie
  March
The Adventures of
  Huckleberry Finn
The Adventures of Tom
  Sawyer
The Aeneid
Agamemnon
The Age of Innocence
The Alchemist (Coelho)
The Alchemist (Jonson)
Alice in Wonderland
All My Sons
All Quiet on the Western
  Front
All the King's Men
All the Pretty Horses
Allen Ginsberg's Poetry
The Ambassadors
American Beauty
And Then There Were
  None
Angela's Ashes
Animal Farm
Anna Karenina
Anthem
Antigone
Antony and Cleopatra
Aristotle's Poetics
Aristotle's Politics
Aristotle: Nicomachean
  Ethics

As I Lay Dying
As You Like It
Astrophil and Stella
Atlas Shrugged
Atonement
The Awakening
Babbitt
The Bacchae
Bartleby the Scrivener
The Bean Trees
The Bell Jar
Beloved
Benito Cereno
Beowulf
Bhagavad-Gita
Billy Budd
Black Boy
Bleak House
Bless Me, Ultima
Blindness
Blood Wedding
The Bloody Chamber
Bluest Eye
The Bonfire of the
  Vanities
The Book of Daniel
The Book of the Duchess
  and Other Poems
The Book Thief
Brave New World
Breakfast at Tiffany's
Breakfast of Champions
The Brief Wondrous Life
  of Oscar Wao
The Brothers Karamazov

The Burning Plain and
  Other Stories
A Burnt-Out Case
By Night in Chile
Call of the Wild
Candide
The Canterbury Tales
Cat on a Hot Tin Roof
Cat's Cradle
Catch-22
The Catcher in the Rye
Cathedral
The Caucasian Chalk
  Circle
Charlotte Temple
Charlotte's Web
The Cherry Orchard
The Chocolate War
The Chosen
A Christmas Carol
Christopher Marlowe's
  Poems
Chronicle of a Death
  Foretold
Civil Disobedience
Civilization and Its
  Discontents
A Clockwork Orange
Coleridge's Poems
The Color of Water
The Color Purple
Comedy of Errors
Communist Manifesto
A Confederacy of
  Dunces
Confessions

For our full list of over 250 Study Guides, Quizzes,
Sample College Application Essays, Literature Essays and E-texts, visit:

www.gradesaver.com

ClassicNotes

GradeSaver™

Getting you the grade since 1999™

Other ClassicNotes from GradeSaver™

Connecticut Yankee in King Arthur's Court
The Consolation of Philosophy
Coriolanus
The Count of Monte Cristo
The Country Wife
Crime and Punishment
The Crucible
Cry, the Beloved Country
The Crying of Lot 49
The Curious Incident of the Dog in the Night-time
Cymbeline
Daisy Miller
David Copperfield
Death in Venice
Death of a Salesman
The Death of Ivan Ilych
Democracy in America
Devil in a Blue Dress
Dharma Bums
The Diary of a Young Girl by Anne Frank
Disgrace
Divine Comedy-I: Inferno
Do Androids Dream of Electric Sheep?
Doctor Faustus (Marlowe)
A Doll's House
Don Quixote Book I

Don Quixote Book II
Dora: An Analysis of a Case of Hysteria
Dr. Jekyll and Mr. Hyde
Dracula
Dubliners
East of Eden
Electra by Sophocles
The Electric Kool-Aid Acid Test
Emily Dickinson's Collected Poems
Emma
Ender's Game
Endgame
The English Patient
The Epic of Gilgamesh
Ethan Frome
The Eumenides
Everyman: Morality Play
Everything is Illuminated
The Faerie Queene
Fahrenheit 451
The Fall of the House of Usher
A Farewell to Arms
The Federalist Papers
Fences
Fight Club
Flags of Our Fathers
Flannery O'Connor's Stories
For Whom the Bell Tolls
The Fountainhead
Frankenstein
Franny and Zooey

The Giver
The Glass Castle
The Glass Menagerie
The God of Small Things
Goethe's Faust
The Good Earth
The Good Woman of Setzuan
The Grapes of Wrath
Great Expectations
The Great Gatsby
Grendel
The Guest
Gulliver's Travels
Hamlet
The Handmaid's Tale
Hard Times
Haroun and the Sea of Stories
Harry Potter and the Philosopher's Stone
Heart of Darkness
Hedda Gabler
Henry IV (Pirandello)
Henry IV Part 1
Henry IV Part 2
Henry V
Herzog
Hippolytus
The Hobbit
Homo Faber
House of Mirth
The House of the Seven Gables
The House of the Spirits
House on Mango Street

For our full list of over 250 Study Guides, Quizzes,
Sample College Application Essays, Literature Essays and E-texts, visit:

www.gradesaver.com

ClassicNotes

GradeSaver™

Getting you the grade since 1999™

Other ClassicNotes from GradeSaver™

How the Garcia Girls
    Lost Their Accents
Howards End
A Hunger Artist
The Hunger Games
I Know Why the Caged
    Bird Sings
I, Claudius
An Ideal Husband
Iliad
The Importance of Being
    Earnest
In Cold Blood
In Our Time
In the Time of the
    Butterflies
Inherit the Wind
An Inspector Calls
Interpreter of Maladies
Into the Wild
Invisible Man
The Island of Dr. Moreau
Jane Eyre
Jazz
The Jew of Malta
Joseph Andrews
The Joy Luck Club
Julius Caesar
The Jungle
Jungle of Cities
Kama Sutra
Kate Chopin's Short
    Stories
Kidnapped
King Lear
King Solomon's Mines

The Kite Runner
Last of the Mohicans
Leaves of Grass
The Legend of Sleepy
    Hollow
A Lesson Before Dying
Leviathan
Libation Bearers
Life is Beautiful
Life of Pi
Light In August
Like Water for Chocolate
The Lion, the Witch and
    the Wardrobe
Little Women
Lolita
Long Day's Journey Into
    Night
A Long Way Gone
Look Back in Anger
Lord Byron's Poems
Lord Jim
Lord of the Flies
The Lord of the Rings:
    The Fellowship of the
    Ring
The Lord of the Rings:
    The Return of the
    King
The Lord of the Rings:
    The Two Towers
A Lost Lady
The Lottery and Other
    Stories
Love in the Time of
    Cholera

The Love Song of J.
    Alfred Prufrock
The Lovely Bones
Lucy
Macbeth
Madame Bovary
Maestro
Maggie: A Girl of the
    Streets and Other
    Stories
Manhattan Transfer
Mankind: Medieval
    Morality Plays
Mansfield Park
The Marrow of Tradition
The Master and
    Margarita
MAUS
The Mayor of
    Casterbridge
Measure for Measure
Medea
Merchant of Venice
Metamorphoses
The Metamorphosis
Middlemarch
A Midsummer Night's
    Dream
Moby Dick
A Modest Proposal and
    Other Satires
Moll Flanders
The Most Dangerous
    Game
Mother Courage and Her
    Children

For our full list of over 250 Study Guides, Quizzes,
Sample College Application Essays, Literature Essays and E-texts, visit:

www.gradesaver.com

ClassicNotes

GrAdeSaver™

Getting you the grade since 1999™

Other ClassicNotes from GradeSaver™

Mrs. Dalloway
Much Ado About
    Nothing
My Antonia
Mythology
The Namesake
Native Son
Never Let Me Go
Nickel and Dimed: On
    (Not) Getting By in
    America
Night
Nine Stories
No Exit
Northanger Abbey
Notes from Underground
O Pioneers
The Odyssey
Oedipus Rex or Oedipus
    the King
Of Mice and Men
The Old Man and the Sea
Oliver Twist
On Liberty
On the Road
One Day in the Life of
    Ivan Denisovich
One Flew Over the
    Cuckoo's Nest
One Hundred Years of
    Solitude
Oroonoko
Oryx and Crake
Othello
Our Town
The Outsiders

Pale Fire
Pamela: Or Virtue
    Rewarded
Paradise Lost
A Passage to India
The Pearl
Percy Shelley: Poems
Perfume: The Story of a
    Murderer
Persepolis: The Story of
    a Childhood
Persuasion
Phaedra
Phaedrus
The Piano Lesson
The Picture of Dorian
    Gray
Poe's Poetry
Poe's Short Stories
Poems of W.B. Yeats:
    The Rose
Poems of W.B. Yeats:
    The Tower
The Poems of William
    Blake
The Poisonwood Bible
Pope's Poems and Prose
Portrait of the Artist as a
    Young Man
The Praise of Folly
Pride and Prejudice
The Prince
The Professor's House
Prometheus Bound
Pudd'nhead Wilson
Purple Hibiscus

Pygmalion
Rabbit, Run
A Raisin in the Sun
The Real Life of
    Sebastian Knight
Rebecca
The Red Badge of
    Courage
The Remains of the Day
The Republic
Rhinoceros
Richard II
Richard III
The Rime of the Ancient
    Mariner
Rip Van Winkle and
    Other Stories
The Road
Robert Frost: Poems
Robinson Crusoe
Roll of Thunder, Hear
    My Cry
Romeo and Juliet
A Room of One's Own
A Room With a View
A Rose For Emily and
    Other Short Stories
Rosencrantz and
    Guildenstern Are
    Dead
Salome
The Scarlet Letter
The Scarlet Pimpernel
The Seagull
Season of Migration to
    the North

For our full list of over 250 Study Guides, Quizzes,
Sample College Application Essays, Literature Essays and E-texts, visit:

www.gradesaver.com

ClassicNotes

GradeSaver™

Getting you the grade since 1999™

Other ClassicNotes from GradeSaver™

Second Treatise of
   Government
The Secret Life of Bees
The Secret River
Secret Sharer
Sense and Sensibility
A Separate Peace
Shakespeare's Sonnets
Shantaram
Short Stories of Ernest
   Hemingway
Short Stories of F. Scott
   Fitzgerald
Siddhartha
Silas Marner
Sir Gawain and the
   Green Knight
Sir Thomas Wyatt:
   Poems
Sister Carrie
Six Characters in Search
   of an Author
Slaughterhouse Five
Snow Falling on Cedars
The Social Contract
Something Wicked This
   Way Comes
Song of Roland
Song of Solomon
Songs of Innocence and
   of Experience
Sons and Lovers
The Sorrows of Young
   Werther
The Sound and the Fury
The Spanish Tragedy

Spenser's Amoretti and
   Epithalamion
Spring Awakening
The Stranger
A Streetcar Named
   Desire
Sula
The Sun Also Rises
Sundiata: An Epic of Old
   Mali
Tale of Two Cities
The Taming of the Shrew
The Tempest
Tender is the Night
Tess of the D'Urbervilles
Their Eyes Were
   Watching God
Things Fall Apart
The Things They Carried
A Thousand Splendid
   Suns
The Threepenny Opera
Through the Looking
   Glass
Thus Spoke Zarathustra
The Time Machine
Titus Andronicus
To Build a Fire
To Kill a Mockingbird
To the Lighthouse
The Tortilla Curtain
Touching Spirit Bear
Treasure Island
Trifles
Troilus and Cressida
Tropic of Cancer

Tropic of Capricorn
Tuesdays With Morrie
The Turn of the Screw
Twelfth Night
Twilight
Ulysses
Uncle Tom's Cabin
Utopia
Vanity Fair
A Very Old Man With
   Enormous Wings
Villette
A Vindication of the
   Rights of Woman
The Visit
Volpone
Waiting for Godot
Waiting for Lefty
Walden
Washington Square
The Waste Land
The Wave
The Wealth of Nations
Where the Red Fern
   Grows
White Fang
A White Heron and
   Other Stories
White Noise
White Teeth
Who's Afraid of Virginia
   Woolf
Wide Sargasso Sea
Wieland
Winesburg, Ohio
The Winter's Tale

For our full list of over 250 Study Guides, Quizzes,
Sample College Application Essays, Literature Essays and E-texts, visit:

www.gradesaver.com

Made in United States
North Haven, CT
06 April 2022

17966030R00161